Working Together for Local Integration of Migrants and Refugees in Barcelona

This document, as well as any data and any map included herein, are without prejudice to the status of or sovereignty over any territory, to the delimitation of international frontiers and boundaries and to the name of any territory, city or area.

Please cite this publication as:
OECD (2018), *Working Together for Local Integration of Migrants and Refugees in Barcelona*, OECD Publishing, Paris.
https://doi.org/10.1787/9789264304062-en

ISBN 978-92-64-30405-5 (print)
ISBN 978-92-64-30406-2 (PDF)

The statistical data for Israel are supplied by and under the responsibility of the relevant Israeli authorities. The use of such data by the OECD is without prejudice to the status of the Golan Heights, East Jerusalem and Israeli settlements in the West Bank under the terms of international law.

Photo credits: Cover © Marianne Colombani

Corrigenda to OECD publications may be found on line at: *www.oecd.org/about/publishing/corrigenda.htm*.

Foreword

An OECD- EU initiative: "Territorial Approach to migrant integration: the role of local authorities"

This publication, "Working together for local integration of migrants and refugees in Barcelona" has been produced by the OECD as part of a larger study entitled "A Territorial Approach to migrant integration: the role of local authorities", which was supported by the European Commission, Directorate General for regional and urban policies.

This study takes stock of the existing multi-level governance frameworks and policies for migrant and refugee integration at the local level in nine large European cities: Amsterdam, Athens, Barcelona, Berlin, Glasgow, Gothenburg, Paris, Rome and Vienna and a small city in Germany (Altena) thanks to the support of the German Ministry for Economic Affairs and Energy. It also builds on information collected from other 61 European cities, including Utrecht, through an ad-hoc survey and on a statistical database on migrant outcomes at regional (TL2) level. This study resulted in the publication of the document entitled "Working together for local integration of refugees and migrants", which was approved by the OECD Regional Development Policy Committee (RDPC) in December 2017 (OECD, 2018).

The focus of this study is on ''migrants'', meaning a wide range of different groups of people with different reasons for leaving their countries of origin: humanitarian, economic, family or study, among others. The target group includes newcomers, from EU and non-EU countries, as well as migrants who settled in the cities many years ago and the native-born with at least one migrant parent[1], depending on the statistical definition used by the city. Given the recent increase in the arrival of refugees and asylum seekers to Europe, particular attention is paid to these groups throughout the case studies.

Cities in the sample have different track records in integrating migrants. The study looks at updates to the governance mechanisms in the wake of the recent influx of asylum seekers and refugees, in order to improve the local reception of migrants and the capacity to integrate them into the society. Conversely, it also investigates opportunities to extend some of the services recently established for newcomers to long-standing migrant groups.

The point of departure for the overall study is the observation that in practice integration takes place at the local level. Cities are focal spots of refugee and migrant reception and integration processes: in 2015, close to two-thirds of the foreign-born population in the OECD lived in urban areas (OECD, 2018).

The ambition of this series of case studies is to identify how cities have responded to these challenges. It aims to address an information vacuum: beyond the dominant

---

[1] See definition of migrant given below.

literature on international and national evidence about migrant movements and integration, several studies exist about the local dimension and impact of migration. However, they do not explore the governance factor attached to it. In the view of partner cities and international organisations (UNHCR, etc.), multi-level governance can be an important explanatory factor of the performance of migrant integration policies. Even though migration policies are the responsibility of the national government, the concentration of migrants in cities, and particularly in metropolitan areas (Boulant, J., M. Brezzi and P. Veneri, 2016; Diaz Ramirez, Liebig, Thoreau and Veneri, 2018), has an impact on the local demand for work, housing, goods and services that local authorities have to manage. Local authorities act within a multi-level budgetary and administrative framework, which limits or adds responsibilities in dealing with migrant-specific impacts in their territory. As such, this work first aims at understanding the way cities and their partners address migrant integration issues. While it does not strive at this stage to evaluate the impact of the whole set of local public actions, it compiles qualitative evidence of city policies, decision making and evaluation processes across selected multi-level governance dimensions and provides a comprehensive perspective on the city's approach to integration. These dimensions were selected according to the multi-level governance gaps analysis developed by the OECD (Charbit, 2011; Charbit and Michalun, 2009). Statistical data have been collected from all of the cities regarding the presence and outcomes of migrant and refugee populations.

As a result of this comparative work, and in collaboration with partner cities and organisations, the OECD compiled a list of key objectives to guide policy makers in integrating migrants with a multi-level perspective. The OECD Checklist for Public Action to Migrant Integration at the Local Level, as included in the Synthesis Report (OECD, 2018) is articulated according to four blocks and 12 objectives. The four blocks cover: 1) institutional and financial settings; 2) time and proximity as keys for migrants and host communities to live together; 3) enabling conditions for policy formulation and implementation; and 4) sectoral policies related to integration (access to the labour market, housing, social welfare and health, and education).

This study first provides insight into Barcelona's migration background and current situation. It then describes the actions implemented following the framework of the "Checklist for public action to migrant integration at the local level".

The objective is to allow cities to learn from each other and to provide national and supranational decision makers and key partners of local integration policies with better evidence to address the major challenges ahead in this field and to adopt appropriate incentive schemes.

Acknowledgements

This publication WORKING TOGETHER FOR LOCAL INTEGRATION OF MIGRANTS AND REFUGEES INBARCELONA was produced by the OECD in partnership with the European Commission as part of a larger study entitled "Territorial approach to migrant integration: The role of local authorities".

This case study has been written by Maria Trullén Malaret, under the supervision of Claire Charbit, Head of the Territorial Dialogue and Migration Unit, and Anna Piccinni, Policy analyst, within the Centre for Entrepreneurship, SMEs, Regions and Cities of the OECD.

This case study has been realised thanks to close collaboration of the municipality of Barcelona who provided the information and organised the OECD field work, as well as the support of the national government officials who provided information. The Secretariat would like to express its gratitude to all participants in the interviews (See Annex 1). In particular to municipal staff members Ramón Sanahuja and Ignasi Calbó for their continuous support throughout the preparation of the case study and to central government representatives Carmen Blanco Gaztañaga and Jose Maria Perez Medina for their guidance. The Secretariat would also like to express its gratitude to Antigone Kotanidis (Athens City Council) for her support as a peer throughout the OECD mission in Barcelona.

The Secretariat is especially thankful for the financial contribution and the collaboration throughout the implementation of the project to the European Union Directorate General for Regional and Urban Policy. In particular we would like to thank Andor Urmos, Louise Bonneau for their guidance as well as for their substantive inputs during the revision of the case study.

Table of contents

Tables

Figures

Boxes

Executive summary

Between 2000 and 2009, the city of Barcelona experienced a rapid increase of international migration. During this process, which was not unique to Barcelona and occurred more broadly in the rest of Spain, Barcelona became a migration hub in the country. The rate of foreign residents in the city has quintupled since 2000. While foreign residents represented 3.5% of Barcelona's population in 2000, they reached 18.1% in 2009. In 2017, 17.5% of the population was foreign, 23% foreign-born and around 30% had a foreign background (AB, 2012; 2016b). While initially, foreign residents were mostly from Latin America, there has been an increase of Asian and European residents in the city. The increase in foreign-born over foreign population is also due to the ease with which Latin American nationals can obtain Spanish nationality (i.e. after 2 years of residency in the country).

The sharp economic crisis and its effects in the labour market widened Barcelona's spatial and socio-economic segregation particularly affecting migrants. Against this context, the city experienced a sharp increase in the number of asylum seeker arrivals: in 2017, the number of asylum claims doubled from 2016. In 2017, after Madrid, Barcelona gathered the highest number of asylum requests submitted in Spain (3 437) which was double the 2016 number (1 650) and triple the 2015 figure (1 143), representing 11.5% of the national share. Still, asylum seeker arrivals remain marginal when compared to other European cities such as Berlin or Athens.

Given the highly decentralised nature of the Spanish institutional and financial setting, a multi-level analysis of integration policies is needed to better mirror how they adapt to territorial specificities. The national government holds key responsibilities for regulating migration and seeking coherence among the mosaic of local integration realities. Subnational governments (i.e. Autonomous Communities and Municipalities) hold key competences for migrant integration. In particular, municipalities with additional competences and capacities, such as Madrid and Barcelona, implement complementary actions to the national ones.

Since late 1990s and until today, the municipality of Barcelona has designed and implemented inclusive measures for migrant integration at the local level. Some benefitted from Barcelona's inclusive implementation of the "Padron" municipal register of inhabitants in Spain. Barcelona developed integration measures around an intercultural vision based on four key strategic principles (1) integrated support and rapid reception of newcomers; (2) equal access to rights and obligations as residents of the city; (3) recognition of diversity as an asset for the city; (4) promotion of interaction among diverse residents to preserve social cohesion. This case study is structured according to the 12 objectives identified in the *OECD Checklist for public action to migrants and refugees integration at the local level*, developed in 2017 through the joint OECD-EU project.

Key findings

Some of the remaining challenges

Employment outcomes: After a period of economic expansion during the 2000s which attracted strong migration flows to the city, non-EU foreign-born people particularly suffered during the economic downturn. This is reflected in the unemployment indicators at the city level showing a ten percentage point gap between foreign residents (23%) and native-born (13.4%) in 2016. This gap reached 41.8% and 20.9% respectively during the peak of the economic crisis in 2013. Further, while Spain's employment performance has improved since the end of the economic crisis, short-term contracts have increased over time and foreigners face poorer labour conditions. This weaker position is partially linked to lower qualification. While employment is not a municipal competence, Barcelona has historically voluntarily developed important labour market integration policies for unemployed and vulnerable residents, including migrants. *Barcelona Activa* plays a key role in developing vocational training, entrepreneurship workshops and matching skills with private sector demand. However, persistent gaps between migrant and native-born suggest that more needs to be done to ease paths into employment and secure long-term and stable professions. Further collaboration between the migration one-stop-shop (SAIER) and *Barcelona Activa* could enhance migrant labour market inclusion.

Access to decent housing: Vulnerable labour market outcomes affect income levels and housing conditions in a context of weak social housing policy with residual public housing (1.5% of the housing stock in Barcelona is public). The main channel to access housing is through the private rental market especially for foreigners who are over-represented in this market. In a tight private rental market, housing affordability in the private sector is a bottleneck for integration, which significantly affects non-EU foreign-born people. Housing costs aggravate migrants' vulnerability and their exposure to social exclusion. Housing affordability is a key priority for the current municipal administration that designed actions to increase long-term affordable housing and more immediate investments in particular to secure housing for refugees. These actions for long-term affordable housing need to be enhanced by all levels of government since housing is a shared responsibility to preserve social cohesion and prevent segregation.

Education obstacles: Migrant pupils are highly concentrated in some schools in the most disadvantaged neighbourhoods (e.g. 40% of pupils in Ciutat Vella are foreign vs. 3.3% in Sarrià Sant Gervasi). Often a high concentration of children of migrants or parents with low education makes learning conditions unequal compared to schools in more prosperous neighbourhoods. Such situations negatively impact both pupils' results and long-term professional perspectives, thus exacerbating long-term inequalities. Further cooperation and sharing the responsibility for welcoming newcomers throughout a city's schools could improve foreign pupils' distribution and achieve better education outcomes.

What is already done and how it could be improved

Multi-level governance: Dialogue on migration matters is ensured between levels of government. The Foreign offices (*Oficinas de Extranjeria*) of the national sub-delegation of the central government in Barcelona and the municipal *Secretariat of Welcome policies for Migrants* are in regular contact to facilitate migrants' administrative procedures (e.g. residency permits, family reunification, etc.). However, Barcelona municipality, like 80% of the 72 cities participating to the OECD study (OECD, 2018), found that limited information sharing and coordination with higher levels of government is the most important governance challenge with regards to integration policies. Lack of coordination is particularly felt with regards to the management of asylum seekers and the refugee reception system. There is no evidence of harmonized access to information across levels of government with regard to decisions on asylum seeker dispersal, allocation criteria and involvement of non-state service providers. Evidence shows that Barcelona, like many other large EU cities analysed in this study, is increasingly called on to address the needs of asylum seekers and recognised refugees who arrive in the city and fall outside of the national reception system. This important reality could be improved through regular dialogue and enhanced coordination (e.g. by anticipating needs of asylum seekers and refugees arriving in the city, improving cost-sharing, etc.) as is done systematically for migration issues. The Netherlands and the Italian SPRAR system could be considered examples of multi-level coordination of reception systems.

Improve the effectiveness of contracts with non-governmental organisations to enhance financial foresight: Like other large cities of the studied sample, the municipality of Barcelona has developed strong coordination mechanisms with a diversity of actors working on migrant integration including (1) NGOs; (2) migrant associations; (3) neighbourhood associations – see point below in "Best Practices that could be replicated". These non-governmental actors implement policies on behalf of the municipality and expand service availability in essential domains such as legal advice, labour market orientation, intercultural activities, language learning or shelter. These partners operate within different forms of financial frameworks. Whereas some have signed bi- or tri-annual contracts with the municipality (i.e. partner NGOs providing essential services outsourced by the municipality in the local migration hub), most of them work through one-off subsidies allocated by different government levels through calls for projects. This method was reported as causing financing and sustainability issues to non-state actors as annual subsidies are disbursed at the end of the year, sometimes pushing NGOs to seek loans in the private market to finance long-term projects upfront.

Capacity and diversity of civil servants: Lack of knowledge and awareness of local civil servants on diversity and migrant specific challenges might curb their access to adequate services. The migration hub (SAIER) delivers migrant-targeted services in 12 different languages and anti-discrimination training (see below the anti-rumour programme). However, the municipality acknowledges the need to further build capacity and diversity beyond front-line services, which are more in relation with migrants (i.e. health, school systems, etc.). By systematically raising awareness on cultural specificities and rights of migrants and refugees among its civil servants, the city will reduce the risk that migrants will experience disruptions or obstacles in accessing public services.

Communication campaign: The municipality's vision and strategies addressing the issue of integration have recognised that the diversity that migrants bring to the community is an asset for the city. Efforts to build public awareness about migration as an asset are clearly recognisable in the Anti-rumours programme. This training on discriminatory behaviours and fake news around migration is offered to public administration staff, citizens and NGOs on a voluntary basis. Some 3 000 anti-rumour volunteers have been trained to fight discrimination. This impressive effort to build a counter-narrative to rumours about migrants and the broader intercultural programme to which it contributes (PROGBI) could benefit from large-scale awareness campaigns via billboards and media coverage. In this sense, the City of Berlin could serve as an example.

Addressing migrant integration at the right scale: Acknowledging that the boundaries of the municipality of Barcelona did not fit with the broader functional urban area, the Barcelona Metropolitan Area (AMB) was created in 2011 uniting 36 neighbouring municipalities. This administrative metropolitan body increasingly manages key policies such as urban planning, environment and transport, yet there is no collaboration between neighbouring local authorities nor within the metropolitan entity on matters regarding migrant integration. Further coordination between neighbouring municipalities with high rates of foreign-born population (e.g. Hospitalet de Llobregat, Santa Coloma de Gramanet, Sant Adrià del Besós, Badalona) could improve migrant integration at the right geographical scale and improve the quality and efficiency of services targeting migrants. Such a cooperative approach, including the joint provision of services and resource sharing, is implemented by the city of Gothenburg for example.

Best practices that could be replicated

Fostering proximity and creating spaces to bring communities together: The municipality considers that the integration process is one of mutual adaptation happening through interaction among different groups. Creating opportunities for this interaction is at the heart of Barcelona's intercultural approach to migrant integration. For instance, the municipality supports intercultural activities through financing of civil society initiatives at the neighbourhood level. Further, public libraries are seen as spaces where interactions among different groups could take place. Attractive libraries are also located in the most disadvantaged areas (e.g. Ciudad Meridiana) and organise activities geared to appeal to the interests of migrant groups (e.g. IT courses to Moroccan women, after-school programmes for children, etc.). They aim to attract different participants and create opportunities to foster interaction among neighbours. Other municipal spaces such as the Espai Avinyó regularly organise intercultural activities (conferences, exhibitions, meetings and concerts about migration and diversity).

Seeking policy coherence at the local level: Since 1998, the municipality has developed a strategy for migrant integration at the local level. A political appointee – the Migration Commissioner - is in charge of municipal action for migrant integration and oversees two secretariats (1) the secretariat of welcome policies for migrants in charge of the reception mechanism, information and front-line services provided to migrants; (2) the secretariat of Citizen rights and diversity which promotes coexistence in diversity, inter-culturalism and anti-discrimination; and (3) Barcelona refugee city which was recently created to improve existing mechanisms for asylum seekers and refugees in the city and is directly linked to the Mayor's office.

Public action over time for migrant integration: The comprehensive welcome system, whose responsibilities mainly fall under the secretariat of welcome policies for migrants, is a unique example of integration policies starting right after migrants' arrival and remaining accessible throughout their lives. The key component of the welcome system is the migration hub (SAIER). This welcome system is accessible to all persons regardless of their legal status. This is in line with the municipality historical approach ensuring access to municipal services to all persons enrolled in the *Padrón*[1]. This inclusive approach also reaches people with no stable address or legal status (e.g. undocumented migrants). The municipality produced, in 2017, an action plan to protect irregular migrants and ease their future integration through support such as employment programmes and language learning as well as information and legal advice on migration.

Participation of migrant residents: Barcelona has a local consultative body, the Municipal Council of Migration, to encourage migrants' presence in the local political sphere and to consult their position in the policy-making process on migrant integration matters enhancing long-term commitment and integration within the city. It is chaired by the Municipal Commissioner of Migration and a representative of a migrant association. Representatives of migrant associations jointly produced a working plan with strategic goals for the 2019 horizon with the municipality and suggested initiatives to achieve them.

Regular coordination with non-state organisations: The municipality works in close collaboration with non-governmental organisations, migrant and neighbourhood associations. Not only are NGOs embedded in municipal structures such as the SAIER but they are also consulted in setting the priorities for integration policies and coordinating their implementation. Platforms such as the Network of Welcome and Support for Migrants, which bring together the municipality and non-governmental actors to enhance coordination and information sharing, have been identified as a best practice for other cities.

A yearly monitoring about local foreign presence and integration outcomes: The administrative municipal census established by the national law (i.e. the *Padrón* registry) allows for an annual assessment of the presence of foreign individuals in the city and is useful in drawing inter-city, regional and national comparisons. Through the *Padrón*, the municipality gathers information about the foreign-born, foreign nationals demographic profile and territorial distribution within the city and educational level of migrants. A yearly municipal report[2] is produced by the municipal department of statistics based on the Padron and other statistical sources, and includes information about the foreign population in the city, which allows local policy makers to better assess migration trends and outcomes for policy design.

Notes

[1] The national law establishes the existence of an administrative municipal census - the *Padron* - managed by the municipality in which every person living in a city must be registered automatically gaining the status of "neighbour" of the municipality regardless of his/her legal status.

[2] The yearly municipal report based produced by the Municipality of Barcelona about Foreigner population in Barcelona:
http://ajuntament.barcelona.cat/bcnacciointercultural/sites/default/files/ficheros/La%20població%20estrangera%20a%20Barcelona%202017.pdf

Key data on migrant presence and integration in Barcelona

Barcelona is the second largest city in Spain with 1 620 809 inhabitants (2017). It is part of the Metropolitan area of Barcelona (3 226 600 inhabitants)[1]; within the province of Barcelona (TL3) (5 533 459 inhabitants) and in the Autonomous Community of Catalonia (TL2) (7 496 276 inhabitants)[2].

Figure 1. Barcelona's location in Spain according to the OECD regional classification

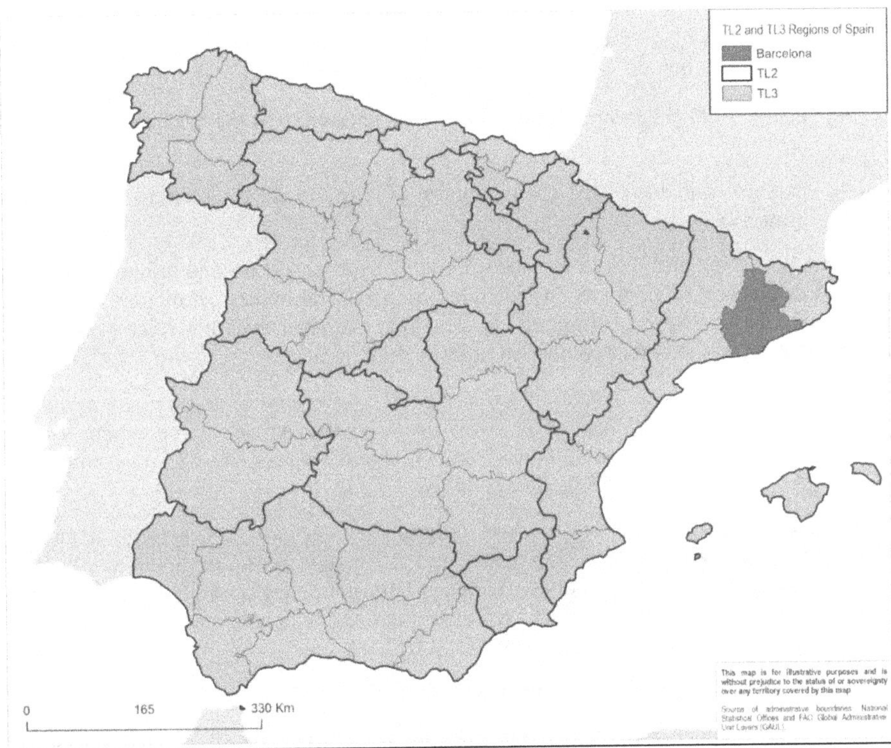

Note: Territorial Level 2 (TL2) consists of the OECD classification of regions within each member country. There are 335 regions classified at this level across 35-member countries. Territorial Level 3 (TL3) consists of the lower level of classification and is composed of 1 681 small regions. In most cases they correspond to administrative regions.
Source: OECD Regional Statistics (database), http://dx.doi.org/10.1787/region-data-en.

Municipality	TL3	TL2	State
Barcelona	Barcelona	Catalonia	Spain

This section presents key definitions and a selection of indicators about migrant presence and integration in Barcelona.

Box 1. Definition of migrant

The term 'migrant' generally functions as an umbrella term used to describe people that move to another country with the intention of staying for a significant period of time. According to the United Nations (UN), a long-term migrant is "a person who moves to a country other than that of his or her usual residence for a period of at least a year (12 months)". Yet, not all migrants move for the same reasons, have the same needs or come under the same laws.

This report considers migrants as a large group that includes:

- Those who have emigrated to an EU country from another EU country ('EU migrants'),

- Those who have come to an EU country from a non-EU country ('non-EU born or third-country national'),

- Those who are foreign-born and obtained host country citizenship through naturalisation;

- Native-born children of immigrants (often referred to as the 'second generation'), and

- Persons who have fled their country of origin and are seeking international protection.

For the latter, some distinctions are needed. While asylum seekers and refugees are often counted as a subset of migrants and included in official estimates of migrant stocks and flows, the UN definition of 'migrant' is clear that the term does not refer to refugees, displaced, or others forced or compelled to leave their homes:

The term 'migrant' in Article 1.1 (a) should be understood as covering all cases where the decision to migrate is taken freely by the individual concerned, for reasons of 'personal convenience' and without intervention of an external compelling factor. (IOM Constitution Article 1.1 (a)).

According to recent OECD work the term "migrant" is a generic term for anyone moving to another country with the intention of staying for a certain period of time – not, in other words, tourists or business visitors. It includes both permanent and temporary migrants with a valid residence permit or visa, asylum seekers, and undocumented migrants who do not belong to any of the three groups (OECD, 2016).

Thus, in this report the following terms are used:

- 'Status holder' or 'refugee' for those who have successfully applied for asylum and have been granted some sort of protection in their host country, including those who are recognised as 'refugees' on the basis of the 1951 Geneva Convection Relating to the Status of Refugees, but also those benefiting from national asylum laws or EU legislation (Directive 2011/95/EU), such as the subsidiary protection status. This corresponds to the category 'humanitarian migrants' meaning recipients of protection – be it refugee status, subsidiary or

- temporary protection – as used in recent OECD work (OECD, 2016). 'Asylum seeker' for those who have submitted a claim for international protection but are awaiting the final decision.

- 'Rejected asylum seeker' for those who have been denied protection status.

- 'Undocumented or irregular migrants' for those who do not have a legal permission to stay.

In Spain, the existence of a local administrative census (Padron) to which residents of a municipality need to be registered regardless of their legal status contributes to providing data on migration trends. It provides information on foreign residents (even when undocumented) based on nationality as well as information on place of birth. The information is provided at different territorial layers (national, autonomous community, province, municipalities and census sections).[3]

Data on asylum applications is gathered at the national and provincial level (TL3) by national authorities. Data of international protection status granted yearly is provided (i.e. refugee and subsidiary protection) yet there is a lack of territorial data on the presence of refugees.

In the case of Barcelona, migrants without permits to stay in the country are referred to as irregular or undocumented migrants.

Source: OECD (2016); UNSD (2017).

Key statistics

The following table contains data for Catalonia (TL2) 2014-2015 and results from an ad hoc extraction from the new database developed by the Economic Analysis, Statistics and Multi-Level Governance Section (CFE) in partnership with the International Migration Division (ELS) of the OECD.

Table 1. Outcomes: Migrant vs. Native population in Catalonia (TL2)

Catalonia (TL2)	Foreign Born in the region (Absolute values)	Foreign Born in the region (% values)	Spanish born in the region (absolute values)	Spanish born in the region (% values)	Foreign born in Spain (absolute values)	Foreign born in Spain (% values)	Spanish born in Spain (abs values	Spanish born in Spain (% values)
A. Presence	1 044 944	14.1	6 352 046	85.9	5 379 292	11.6	41 070 308	88.4
B. Employment	368 478	53.7	2 693 335	64.6	1 016 500	57.7	13 995 480	53.5
C. Unemployment	171 870	31.8	535 864	16.6	203 420	16.7	2 261 060	13.9
D. Overqualification	57 572	15.6	462 919	17.2	152 176	15	2 157 133	15.4
E. Primary	357 104	52.1	1 728 955	41.5	1 071 780	56.4	21 761 460	66.4
F. Secondary	154 388	22.5	858 340	20.6	428 960	22.6	5 097 920	15.6
G. Tertiary	174 208	25.4	1 580 965	37.9	401 300	21.1	5 902 300	18
H. Rooms per capita		1.3		1.9		1.5		1.8
I. Immigration good for country's economy (0 to 10)				4.8				5.1
K. Dependency ratio		10.4		38.5		10.8		36.3

Note: The following definitions apply to the table above
Source: OECD database on migrant population outcome at TL2 level.

Definition	Absolute values	Relative values
A. Presence	Total	Share on total population (0+ years old)
B. Employment	Total	Employment rate (%):employed individuals as a percentage of total working-age population (15-64 years old)
C. Unemployment	Total	Unemployment rate (%):unemployed individuals as a percentage of total labour force (15-64 years old)
D. Overqualification	Total of those individuals with "high" level of education and in low or medium skilled jobs	Overqualification rate (%):overqualified workers as a percentage of total employed (15-64 years old)
E. Primary	Total with primary education	As a percentage of total working age population (%) (ages 15-64 and excluding those currently in education or training)
F. Secondary	Total with secondary education	
G. Tertiary	Total with tertiary education	
H. Rooms per capita		Average number or rooms per inhabitant
I. Immigration good for country's economy (0 to 10)		Average value on the scale 0 to 10, where 10 is the most positive opinion
J. Allow immigrants of different race/ethnic group?	Total	Total percentage of people who believe immigrants should be allowed into the country (%)
K. Dependency ratio		Dependent population (0-14 & 65+ years old) as a percentage of total population (0+ years old) (%)

Background information

City composition

There are 10 municipal districts - the highest territorial unit within the municipality - and 73 neighbourhoods in Barcelona. According to the Statistics of Barcelona (2016), the districts with the highest percentage of foreign born are Ciutat Vella (42.8%), l'Eixample (18.6%) and Sants Montjuic (18.6%). Some neighbourhoods in the districts of Nou Barris (i.e. Ciutat Meridiana; Trinitat Vella) and Sant Martí (i.e. el Besós i el Maresma) concentrate more foreign-born people than the average.

Figure 2. The 73 neighbourhoods of Barcelona

Source: Municipality of Barcelona

Subnational government expenditure as a % of GDP

In 2017 subnational government expenditure accounted for 20.8% of GDP (OECD average is 16.2%) and 49.2% of public expenditure (OECD average is 40.4%) (Source: OECD, 2018) Database on subnational governments and finance).

Subnational governments' public expenditure

Subnational governments in Spain are responsible for 49.2% of public expenditure (OECD average is 40.4%) (OECD, 2018) Database on subnational governments and finance).

Population trends in Barcelona

- **Total City Population:** 1 620 809 inhabitants (INE, 2017).

- **Percentage of foreign population:** in 2016, 267 790 foreign residents, which accounted for 16.6% of the total population. Of those foreign residents 31% come from EU countries while 63.9% come from non-EU countries (Idescat, 2016).

- **Percentage of foreign-born**: 23.7% (Idescat, 2017).

- **Number of irregular migrants:** Estimated around 10 000 - 15 000 (Ajuntament de Barcelona, 2017a)

- **Number of unaccompanied minors:** 122 (Ajuntament de Barcelona, 2017b)

- **The biggest countries of origin:** In order of importance in 2015: Italy (10.08% of all migrants), Pakistan (7.2%), China (6.9%), France (5.1%), Morocco (4.7%), Bolivia, Ecuador, Philippines, Peru, Colombia. 150 nationalities live in the city. (Statistics of Barcelona, 2016).

- **Number of asylum seekers and recognised refugees:** There is no precise data about the number of asylum seekers and refugees in the municipality of Barcelona. According to the Oficinas de Extranjeria of the Sub-delegation of the Government in Barcelona, at the provincial level (Tl3) 1 650 asylum seekers claimed asylum in 2016. It was a 42% increase since 2015. The number of people using the municipal social services for matters related to asylum was higher: 2 292 in 2016 (e.g. people having moved to Barcelona after having claimed asylum somewhere else). Asylum seekers primarily hail from Venezuela, Ukraine, El Salvador and Syria.

Employment trends for migrants

- **The main industrial sectors where migrants work**: Wholesale and retail trade; Accommodation and food service activities; Domestic work and personal care (e.g. maids, elderly -care; Construction

- **Employment by type of contract:** Spanish people: 20.5% fixed-term contracts and 79.5% unlimited-term contracts; Foreign people: 22.9% fixed-term contracts and 66.1% unlimited-term contracts.

- **Unemployment:**

Table 2. Unemployment rate by nationality, percentages (%, TL3 level, Barcelona)

	2008	2013	2016
Spanish and dual nationality	6.1	20.9	13.4
Foreign	11.7	41.8	23
Total	7.1	24.4	14.7

Source: IERMB (2018); Based on microdata from the EPA- INE.

- **Share of self-employment:**

Table 3. Share of self-employment at the national level in Spain (2015)

	% of Active Population that is self-employed	% of Occupied Population that is self-employed
Total population self-employment	12.7	16.2
Nationals	11.4	14.6
EU Citizens	0.6	0.7
Non-EU citizens	0.7	0.9

Source: Eurostat (database).

- **Over-qualification rate:** At the regional level (TL2): Foreign-born over-qualification reached 15.62%; Native-born over-qualification 17.19% (OECD database)

Educational attainment

Table 4. Education attainment rate (%) by nationality in Barcelona (2011)

Level of education	Spanish	Foreign
No studies	7.5	2.1
Primary	11.7	22.7
Junior High	20.8	18.1
High School or vocational training	28.1	21.1
Higher learning and University	32	36

Source: Author's elaboration from Ajuntament de Barcelona (2016b).

Net annual migrant household income in the municipality of Barcelona

- **Percentage of the median equalised disposable income of the total population in Barcelona:** Total (nationalities)=100; Spanish=104.5; Rest of the EU=93.4; Latin America=58.2; Rest of the world=49.7(Municipal Statistics of Ajuntament de Barcelona)

Population at risk of poverty

- At the municipal level, for 2011: Catalan-born at risk of poverty: 17.6%; foreign-born residents at risk of poverty: 19%.

- Housing burden is important for foreign-born. When considering housing costs: Catalan-born at risk of poverty: 16.4%; foreign-born at risk of poverty: 29.6% (Source: Municipal Statistics of Ajuntament de Barcelona)

Right to vote

- Residents with EU nationality and from Bolivia, Colombia, Ecuador, Norway, New Zealand, Paraguay, Peru, and Chile can vote in municipal elections.

Notes

[1] The Metropolitan Area of Barcelona approximately corresponds to a Functional Urban Area according to OECD definition. The OECD definition of functional urban areas uses population density to identify urban cores and travel-to-work flows to identify the hinterlands whose labour market is highly integrated with the cores. The Barcelona FUA is slightly more populous than the Metropolitan Area: 3 846 697 residents in 2014.

[2] Territorial Level 2 (TL2) consists of the OECD classification of regions within each member country. There are 335 regions classified at this level across 35 member countries. Territorial

Level 3 (TL3) consists of the lower level of classification and is composed of 1 681 small regions. In most cases they correspond to administrative regions.

[3] www.ine.es/dyngs/INEbase/es/operacion.htm?c=Estadistica_C&cid=1254736177012&menu=ulti Datos&idp=1254734710990 ; www.ine.es/prensa/cp_2017_p.pdf.

Introduction

The increase of international migration in Europe has enhanced public interest about how governments promote the integration of newcomers into host societies. While Spain has not been one of the countries receiving the highest number of newcomers during the most recent spike in arrivals to Europe, the country, and notably the city of Barcelona, experienced for the last fifteen years a sharp increase in migrant arrivals, which required a rapid adaptation from the different levels of government. The objective of this case-study is to provide an analysis of migrant integration and related multilevel governance mechanisms in Barcelona. Integration takes time and the implementation of appropriate measures, while success will benefit both migrants and the host society. The implementation of appropriate policies requires coordination among different levels of government and the wide array of actors involved.

There are diverse and complementary dimensions of migrant integration in host societies which require the involvement of many policy fields (e.g. access to the labour market, housing, education, social, cultural, etc.) (Schnapper, 2007). Integration is also understood to be a two-way process affecting both people with migration backgrounds and society as a whole, and hence integration is not only about a specific population but also about the response and inclusiveness of the host society (Schnapper, 2007).

A central tenet of this report is the focus on multi-level governance. An effective multi-level governance of public policies depends on the relations among public actors at different levels of government (vertical), but also within the relevant administrations (horizontal), as well as with non-governmental actors (Charbit, 2011). A coordinated public action of policies and programmes is an essential component to achieve the desired outcomes of the policy (Idem).

Migration has traditionally been approached as a national prerogative considered emblematic of national sovereignty and the State capacity to control its borders (in the context of increased Europeanisation of migration policies) (Giraudon, 2009). Migrant integration, on the other hand, has been layered at various levels of government including supranational, national and subnational governments with non-governmental stakeholders heavily involved (Scholten and Penninx, 2016). Local authorities are at the forefront in providing essential local public services for migrant and vulnerable migrant groups and have played an essential role in the design and implementation of short- and long-term responses favouring migrant integration (Scholten, 2014). Indeed, it is at the local level that integration takes place. Municipal governments, particularly in cities, design and adapt their integration programmes in response to the local context (Scholten, 2014).

Barcelona, like other European cities, proactively responded to the increase in arrivals by mobilising its migrant integration services and has recently adapted them in response to the surge in arrivals of asylum seekers. Since the late 1990s, the municipality of Barcelona has been implementing a strategic intercultural approach to migrant integration based on egalitarian and cultural freedom principles, while emphasising the need for interaction among different cultural groups (Zapata, 2015). In Spain, the multi-level character of migrant integration is shaped by the decentralised nature of the country. Spain devolves many important competences to regions (or "Autonomous Communities") while increased competences are allocated to the cities of Madrid and Barcelona. Competences relevant to migrant integration are both subnational and national ones. The national government plays an essential role in regulating migration flows and coordinating the vast diversity of subnational approaches to integration.

The report is based on (1) an extensive questionnaire designed by the OECD and completed by the municipality of Barcelona in the beginning of 2017; (2) reports and studies produced by official authorities, the OECD and private institutions; (3) research papers conducted by academics; (4) statistics from the INE, Idescat, Municipal Statistics and the OECD, in particular the OECD statistical database on migrant outcomes at TL2 level which is one of the outcome of this project; (5) interviews conducted by the OECD field mission in April 2017 with representatives of the municipality and partner stakeholders including representatives of national and regional governments as well as civil society and migrants and (6) complementary information from national and local authorities.

The following case study about the city of Barcelona is organised in two sections. A first section takes a snapshot of migration in the city, including current migrant populations, historic migrant and refugee flows and nationalities, key laws and the main challenges emerging in the city related to migrant integration. The second part presents the policy responses to migrant integration issues in Barcelona. These actions are presented according to the objectives identified in the OECD "Checklist for Public Action to migrant integration at the local level" (OECD, 2018). The first block of the Checklist presents the multi-level governance setting that applies to Barcelona's integration policy; the institutional mapping helps to clarify the allocation of competences across levels of government. The second block describes how integration solutions are designed over time and aim to create close collaboration among all groups. The third block overviews operational, capacity building and monitoring tools used by the city for policy implementation. The last block introduces sectoral actions to facilitate integration through labour market, education, housing and social services.

Chapter 1. Migration Snapshot of the city of Barcelona

Barcelona (Ajuntament de Barcelona) is the second most populated city in Spain with more than 1 620 809 inhabitants. It is the most populated city of the region (Autonomous Community of Catalonia) which includes 7.5 million people. There are provinces within the Autonomous Communities (4 provinces in Catalonia, for example) and the city of Barcelona is part of the province of Barcelona (TL3) and is at the heart of a metropolitan area of 3.2 million residents. In the City there are ten municipal districts - the most granular territorial and administrative unity - and 73 neighbourhoods in the metropolitan area. In 2018, relevant competences for migrant integration are the remit of central, regional and local governments whereas provincial and metropolitan bodies do not have competences in terms of migrant integration and do not implement policies pertaining to it. Yet, the provincial level remains used for statistical purposes.

Migration insights in the city of Barcelona: flows, populations and legislation

A territorial approach to migration: Barcelona as a migration hub in Spain

As an industrial city and a Mediterranean port, Barcelona has traditionally been a migrant destination.

Contemporary Barcelona is the result of two key inflows of newcomers, the first resulting from internal mobility at the country level and the second from international migration. The first one followed the Spanish Civil War and post-war period. In the 1950s and 1960s, Barcelona's industrial economy attracted large inflows of low-skilled workers from the south and west of Spain, which contributed to the city's economic growth. Indeed, in 1975, 44% of the residents were born outside Catalonia and were working mainly in the industrial and care sectors. The inflows of international migration remained low and emigration - rather than immigration - was more prevalent in Spain across the country.

Secondly, since the early 2000s and until 2009, the city of Barcelona experienced a rapid increase of international migration. This process was not unique to Barcelona and occurred more broadly in Catalonia and the rest of Spain but the rate of foreign residents in the city is higher than regional and national rates. The number of foreigners living in the city has quintupled since 2000. While foreign residents accounted for 3.5% of Barcelona's residents in 2000, they reached 18.1% in 2009. In 2010, after the economic crisis, the amount of arrivals decreased. In 2016, 16.6% of the city's population was foreign, 23% was born abroad (including foreign-born who have been naturalised and obtained Spanish citizenship) and around 30% had a foreign background (AB, 2012; AB, 2016b) (See Table 1.1; See Figure 1.1).

Table 1.1. Changes in population of foreign residents at local, regional and national levels

	Barcelona		Catalonia	Spain
	Absolute numbers	Foreign as a % of total population	Foreign as a % of total population	Foreign as a % of total population
2000	53 428	3.5%	2.9%	2.3%
2005	230 942	14.2%	11.4%	9.5%
2010	284 632	17.6%	16%	12.5%
2016	267 790	16.6%	13.6%	9.9%

Source: Idescat (n.d.), *Padró Municipal d'habitants, Local census* (Database). AB (2004 ; 2008 ; 2016)

The factors driving international migration in the late 1990s and early 2000s were the economic growth and expansive labor market of the period. The labour market, which has a substantial informal sector (notably in personal care, construction and tourism), easily absorbed undocumented migrants soon after their arrival. In the 2000s, around 20% of national GDP was generated by the underground economy (Schneider, 2010). Lastly, the image of Barcelona as a cosmopolitan city is also a contributing factor to immigration. The presence of foreign people from EU-28 countries has increased both in relative and absolute terms even amid the economic crisis (AB, 2016b). Barcelona is highly attractive for international students with 8 476 foreign students registered in Barcelona's universities in 2016, mainly from Europe and Latin America.

Figure 1.1. Spanish and Foreign (%), Barcelona

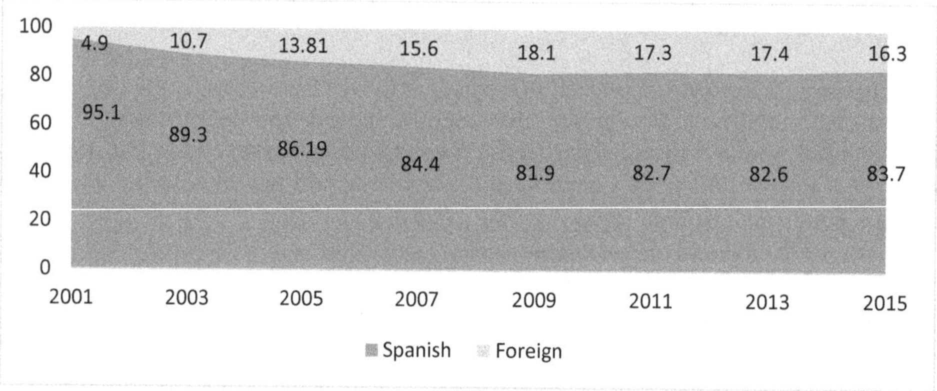

Source: Statistics of Barcelona (AB 2004; 2008; 2016), *Municipal Padron* (database).

Foreign residents have a highly diverse national background. While initially foreign residents were mostly from Latin America, there has been an increase in Asian and European residents in the city. In fact, the number of Latin American migrants has decreased in absolute terms. This should be understood through a two-folded explanation: not only are there are fewer Latin American nationals arriving in Barcelona but, in addition, they can obtain Spanish nationality faster than other groups. In fact, Latin American nationals can apply for citizenship after two years of residency, refugees after 5 years and all other nationalities after 10 years of legal residence. In practice, and to give an example, it means that while there are 8 108 Ecuadorians in the city, the number of residents born in Ecuador is almost triple: there are 23 546 Barcelona residents who were born in Ecuador. The foreign-born population in the city is 23.7% of the total population and the main countries of birth are Ecuador (6.5%), Peru (6.3%), Argentina (5.8%) and Pakistan (5.4%). Policies addressing integration, which is a long-term process, should continue to target such groups (See Table 1.2 and Table 1.3).[1]

Table 1.2. Changes in population of foreign residents by origin, Barcelona

Foreign Nationalities (Main countries)	2007	2016
Asia (Pakistan, China)	42 568	67 494
Europe (Italy, France)	68 547	96 646
North Africa (Morocco)	15 249	15 003
Sub-Saharan Africa (Senegal)	3 831	4 055
North, Central America and Caribbean (Honduras, Dominican Republic)	12 245	25 455
South America (Bolivia, Ecuador)	99 968	58 061
Total Foreign Residents	250 789	267 790

Source: Statistics of Barcelona (2016), Municipal Padron (database).

Table 1.3. Residents by country of birth, Barcelona, 2017

	Total Population	Native born	Foreign born
Absolute number	1 625 137	1 239 256	2 620
Percentage of total	100	76.3%	23.7%

Source: Department of Statistics, Barcelona City Council

During the 2000s, a common procedure of arrival was through family reunification but the economic crisis caused a decline in these applications (See Table 1.4).

Table 1.4. Change in Number of Applications for Family Reunification in Barcelona

	2007	2011	2015
Number of applications	6 943	3 446	2 620
1st nationality (% of total)	Ecuador (18. 9%)	Pakistan (16.3%)	Pakistan (23.4%)
2nd nationality (% of total)	Peru (11%)	Bolivia (11.1%)	China (10.5%)

Note: Family reunification is the process that non-EU foreign residents need to undertake to bring to Barcelona their nuclear family. It is normatively framed by the Directive 2003/86 of the European Commission about the right to family reunification and the articles 16-17 of the Spanish Organic law 4/2000 about the rights and liberties of foreign residents and to participate the foreign resident needs to prove residency for longer than a year, adequate housing conditions to reunify the family as well as sufficient economic resources.
Source: Statistics of Barcelona (2007; 2016), Municipal Padron (database).

An overview of Spanish legislation applicable to foreigners

Since Spain was a country of emigration rather than immigration until the late 1990s, the definition of specific jurisdictional powers and a correspondent policy framework for migrant integration was not a priority until then. The first Spanish law on rights of migrants was approved in 1985.

Progressively, the regulatory framework has been adapted. Essential Spanish legislation is established in the *LO 4/2000 Organic law about Rights and Liberties of foreigners in Spain* and their integration. The law has been reformed according to EU regulations and labour market developments (key reforms in 2004, 2009, 2012).

In the short history of immigration in Spain, migrant regulation has been approached through employment lenses and placed under the control of the Ministry of Employment and Social Security. An essential characteristic of the LO 4/ 2000 is the orderly control of migrant workers in accordance with the needs of the national employment situation The LO 4/2000 specifies rights and obligations of foreign residents at the national level. Foreigners with a resident permit have equal access to all public services. Regardless of legal status, all foreigners under the age of 16 are guaranteed access to education. After a 2012 reform, universal access to health is only granted to vulnerable migrants except in emergencies.

This essential law regulates both entrance and residency. There are three forms of permits: reunification, work and residence permits[2]. While considered an exceptional procedure by law, the common procedure to obtain an initial permit is through the "Arraigo" method which means "Rooting": the applicant needs to prove permanent residence over three years (through the Padron register), a signed job contract of at least a year and a report proving social ties emitted by the regional government as well reports proving absence of criminal records. References to the *"Arraigo"* procedure will be made throughout this case study. Studies show that this type of undocumented or irregular experience is common among non-EU migrants: 40% of migrants living in Spain have spent a period of irregularity on the national territory along their migration path and a clear majority entered the country without a working permit, although this various depending on country of origin (Gonzalez Enriquez, 2009). Often migrants remain irregular for a period of three years, during this time they work in the informal sector (i.e. construction, domestic and care work) but remain excluded from non-municipal public services (i.e. employment, welfare, housing). After three years they can access the *Arraigo* procedures.

With the 2009 reform, Autonomous Communities (Spain's regional authorities) are entitled to grant initial *work permits* according to national law. The competence to authorise entry and stay (i.e. deliver residence permits) remains at the national level. The 2009 reform also assigns to Autonomous Communities and Municipalities the task of producing "reports" assessing migrant efforts to integrate in Spain which are required for the *"Arraigo"* procedure to obtain work and residence permits. Local authorities are also in charge of issuing 'housing adequacy' reports, which area required for family reunification procedures.

Long-term permits are not accessible until a minimum of 5 years after the initial residence and work permit are obtained, requiring a series of short renewals of work permits and continuous periods of temporary legal status.

It is worth mentioning that migrant regulation and control which is an exclusively national competence, is a policy domain in which national and municipal government levels do not converge in terms of objectives.

An overview of asylum flows in Spain and the city of Barcelona

In 2017, asylum requests in Spain rose sharply, an increase that had already started in previous years. Still, asylum seeker arrivals in the country remain marginal when compared to neighbouring countries. In 2016, there were 15 755 asylum claims, and in 2017, 31 563 which represents an annual increase of 91%. The countries of origin of asylum seekers are also divergent from European peers linked to historical connections with Latin America: in 2017 the vast majority was from Venezuela (10 511) followed by Syria (4 271) and Colombia (2 487).

Figure 1.2. Changes in the number of asylum claims in Spain

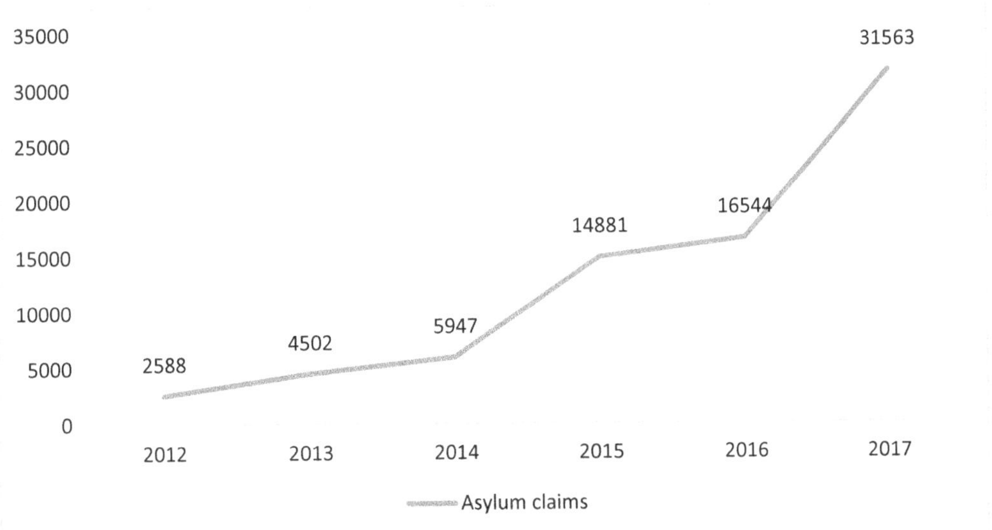

Source: Eurostat and Ministry of Interior (database).

In Spain, out of the 13 350 decisions taken in 2017 (which do not refer to 2017 applications since the average asylum procedure lasts 14.4 months), 65% were rejected and 35% were accepted. Among the 4 675 positive responses, 4 080 received subsidiary protection and 595 refugee status in 2017. (Eurostat, CEAR, 2018; ACCEM, 2017). In line with the findings of this OECD study, the key question pertains to the irregular status of rejected asylum-seekers, who are asked to leave the country but often decide to remain in situation of irregularity specially since the asylum procedure lasts more than a year on average, or to irregularly cross the borders to another EU country.

Barcelona has participated in the national trend as asylum claims have increased markedly in the last five years, while remaining considerably lower compared to other European cities participating in this OECD sample. In 2017, after Madrid, Barcelona received the most asylum requests in Spain (3 437). This was a three-fold increase on 2015 data (See Figure 1.3). In 2016, the main countries of origin of asylum seekers in the city were Venezuela (339) followed by Ukraine (280), El Salvador (88) and Syria (74). Barcelona's municipal migration hub (SAIER) welcomed 2 292 asylum seekers in 2016 (in 2015: 1 372; in 2014: 811; in 2013: 423; in 2012: 304).

Figure 1.3. Changes in the Number of Asylum claims in Barcelona province (TL3)

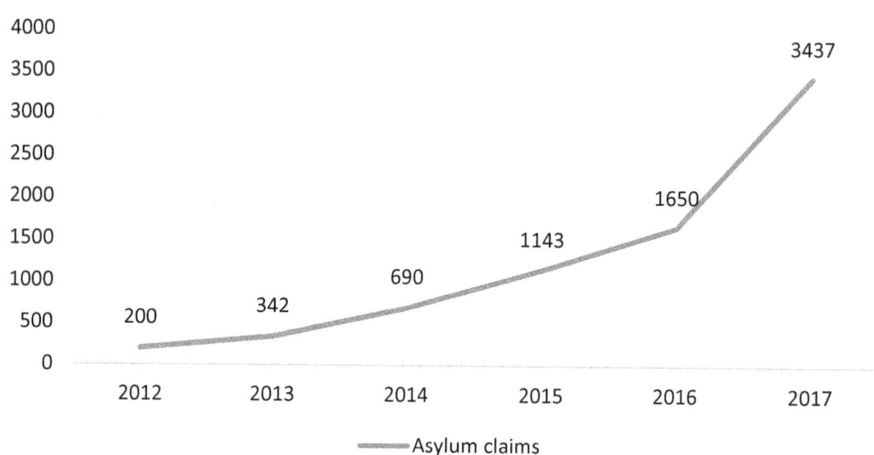

Source: Dirección General de Política Interior; Sub-delegación del gobierno en Barcelona, Oficinas de Extranjería (2017)

City well-being and inclusion

The following section presents some integration outcomes while describing both the economic characteristics of Barcelona and some residential and social issues that characterise the city.

An overview of the city's economic context

92% of Barcelona's residents are satisfied with the city and neighbourhoods in which they live, which is one of the highest rates in Europe (European Commission, 2016).

Barcelona, the second most important city in Spain in economic terms, has a dynamic economy and world class reputation with qualities that enabled it to withstand the economic crisis (OECD, 2009; OECD, 2010a). In Barcelona's diversified economy, tertiary activities are the most prevalent (90% of the workforce). The relative weight of industry has decreased (7% of the workforce)[3]. The touristic sector is important in terms of employment as Barcelona is the third most-visited city in Europe (19.5 million overnight stays in 2016). During the 2000s, the construction sector was pivotal in driving the expansive labour market but was sharply affected by the crisis. Barcelona is attracting more international investment and becoming a European start-up hub. According to the 2018 Digital Start-up Ecosystem Overview, Barcelona has consolidated as a technological hub in the south of Europe and the 5th largest European tech hub after London, Paris, Berlin and Dublin.

Since the 1980s and until the economic crisis, Barcelona's labour market was expansive. After 2007, the economic crisis, which hit Spain particularly hard, hurt Barcelona's labour market. The unemployment rates picked up from 8.8% in 2001 to 15% in 2016 having reached 23.5% in 2013. Still, Barcelona's labour market fared better during the economic crisis than the national average (See Table 1.5 and Figure 1.4).

**Table 1.5. Activity and Occupation rates at different levels,
2014, 4th quarter**

	Activity	Occupation
Barcelona	80.8%	71.4%
Catalonia	78.5%	66.8%
Spain	75.1%	61%

Source: INE, *Survey of Active Population* (database).

Figure 1.4. Changes in unemployment rates 2000-2016, Country and city level

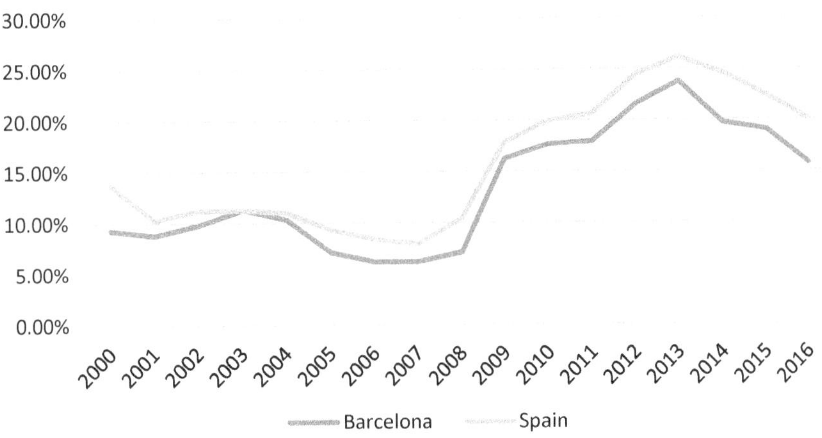

Source: INE, *Survey of Active Population* (database).

Along with unemployment a key outcome of the crisis has been the increased duality of the labour market with an increase of short-term contracts (77% indefinite-term contracts and 23% temporary contracts in 2015) (AB, 2017c). In this context, foreign residents who occupy vulnerable positions in the labour market are severely affected by unemployment and labour insecurity (See Objective 9).

Segregation and inequalities in Barcelona

The economic crisis and its labor market effects exacerbated territorial and socio-economic inequalities in Barcelona (IERMB-AMB-DIBA-IDESCAT, 2014).

Worsening income inequalities particularly affecting migrant residents

Income inequalities widened in the wake of the economic crisis. The evolution of the Gini index of household disposable income illustrates the socio-economic polarisation after the crisis. While between 1985 and 2006 income inequalities decreased in Barcelona (i.e. positive progression of the Gini index from 0.4 to 0.3), they increased following the economic crisis and the percentage of households with a low and very-low HDI has sharply increased since 2007 (Table 1.6) (AMB, 2014).

Table 1.6. Distribution of population by level of Household Disposable Income (HDI), Barcelona

HDI/Year	2007	2010	2014
Very low	4.1%	12.1%	15.5%
Low	17.6%	25.7%	21.1%
Medium-low	38.2%	28.3%	29.3%
Medium-high	20.3%	18.1%	17.5%
High	12.2%	8%	5%
Very high	7.5%	7.8%	11.6%

Source: Ajuntament de Barcelona (2015), *PDH 2016-2025*.

Income gaps between foreign residents, in particular women, and Spanish nationals (See Table 1.7) have formed since the crisis has deepened.

Table 1.7. Average income by nationality and gender, Barcelona 2014

	Average income (In euros)	Men	Women
Total (Nationality)	28 649	32 868	24 618
Spanish	29 946	34 784	25 511
Rest of the EU	26 747	31 274	21 604
Latin America	16 670	19 293	14 476
Rest of the world	14 250	14 709	13 482

Source: Barcelona City Hall, Department of Statistics.

The economic crisis not only increased inequalities but also monetary poverty, which affected 18.3% of Barcelona's residents in 2011 (last data available) (AMB, 2012). At the national level, foreign-born people in Spain have the second highest rate of relative poverty in the OECD (40%) and their probability to be poor doubles versus that of the native-born (OECD-EU, 2015). In Barcelona, among the impoverished residents, foreign residents are also over-represented. The rate of foreigners threatened by poverty is higher than the national average. Besides, the structure of the Spanish housing system (e.g. traditional promotion of homeownership and residual public housing) particularly affects foreigners. Housing is an important bottleneck for migrant integration in Barcelona: housing highly increases the risk of poverty for foreign born reaching 30%, whereas it decreases the one of Spanish-born (See Table 10). Such a housing over-burden for foreign-born can be linked to higher difficulties in accessing credit, housing bubbles and reliance on family in the Spanish welfare and housing system (See Objective 10).

Table 1.8. Risk of poverty by geographical origin, Barcelona 2011

	Rate of risk of poverty	Rate of risk of poverty when considering rents
Total	18.6%	16.4%
Catalonia	17.6%	12.9%
Rest of Spain	20.7%	10.9%
Rest of the world	19%	29.6%

Source: Barcelona City Hall, Department of Statistics.

Spatial segregation in the city of Barcelona

The economic crisis widened spatial segregation by income within the city as in other metropolitan areas in the developed world including European cities (OECD, 2016).

Across Barcelona's neighbourhoods, the unemployment rate is unevenly distributed ranging from 3.1 % (Vallvidrera- Tibidabo) to 16.5% (La Marina del Prat Vermell) (See Figure 1.5). These divergent labour market outcomes translate into wide income inequalities by neighbourhood, which have sharpened following the crisis. While in 2008, the household disposable income of the richest neighbourhood was 4.3 times higher than the one from the poorest neighbourhood, in 2015, the richest neighbourhood was 7.3 times richer than the poorest one (Ciutat Meridiana) (AB, 2016c) (See Figure 1.6).

Figure 1.5. Unemployment spatial disparities by neighbourhood

Unemployment level by neighbourhood (as a %)

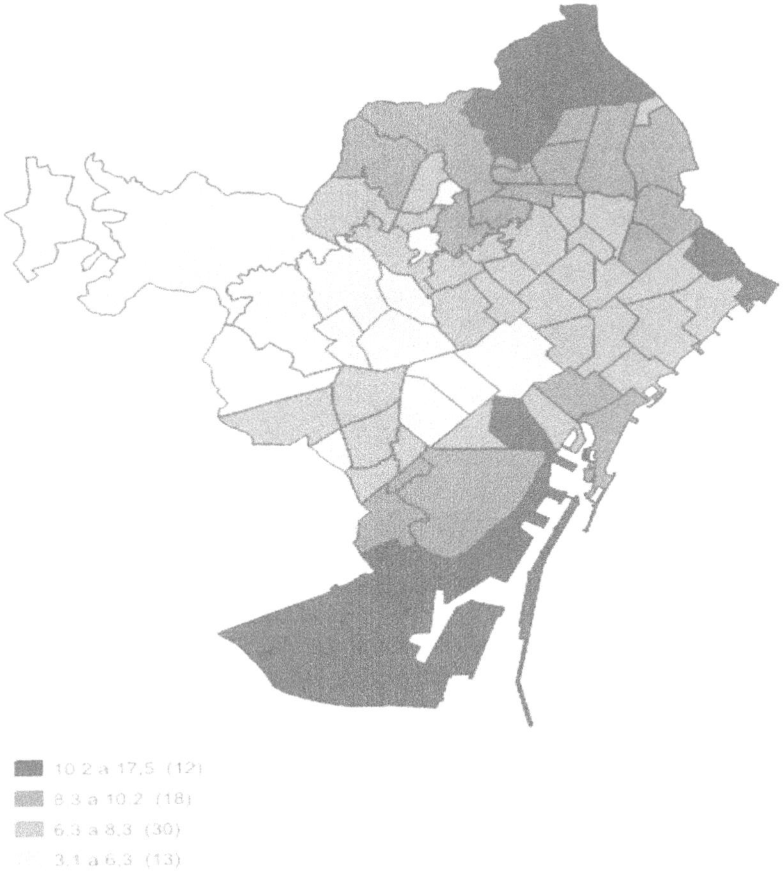

Source: Ajuntament de Barcelona, Estadístiques.

Figure 1.6. Income inequalities by neighbourhood

Household disposable income in 2015, Index 100

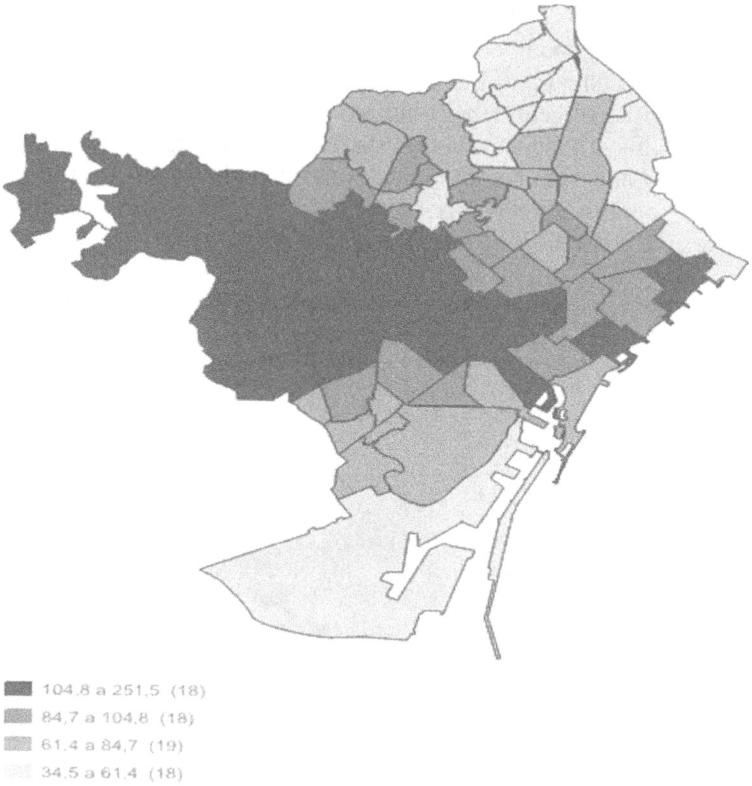

Source: Estadístiques de Barcelona.

Within the diverse and multidisciplinary research on segregation, research on the unequal spatial distribution of migrants and non-migrants within urban areas occupy a central position (Massey, 1985). Following rising migration in Barcelona in the 2000s, academic research analysed the localisation of immigrant housing within the city and its metropolitan area. The existence of the municipal local administrative census – the *Padron* – facilitates the monitoring and its accuracy since migrants can register regardless of their status and indicate their address.

Urban segregation indexes are low in Barcelona (Bayona and Lopez, 2011) and the overall spatial distribution of migrants within the city appears to be relatively homogenous (i.e. between 11% and 19% of the population of almost every district). However, two main areas of the city concentrate bigger migrant groups. First, the historical downtown of Barcelona – Ciutat Vella – which has played a central function as a gateway for migrants since the 1990s (Martinez, 1999; Pareja-Eastaway, 2009; Bayona and Lopez, 2011). The district of Ciutat Vella concentrates some of the neighbourhoods with higher rates of foreign residents (i.e. EL Raval 48.5%, Barri Gotic 43.2%). Second, some peripheral neighbourhoods of the city, having historically received cohorts of internally mobile workers, increasingly attracted more migrants (e.g. Ciutat Meridiana in Nou Barris 27.5%).

There are strong disparities on spatial distribution patterns between EU and non-EU foreign nationals. EU nationals generally live in areas with high housing prices (e.g. Eixample) whereas non-EU nationals are located in neighbourhoods were the household's disposable income is lower and housing more affordable (e.g. Ciutat Meridiana in Nou Barris). Ciutat Vella is a counter-example. The historical downtown was traditionally affordable and concentrates the higher rate of foreigners in the city, but housing prices have been rocketing recently due to strong international interest in the city from tourists; as a result, real estate investors have been pushing low-income residents towards more peripheral areas (See Figure 1.7; See Table 1.9; See Objective 10).

Figure 1.7. Distribution of foreign residents at the neighbourhood level, 2016

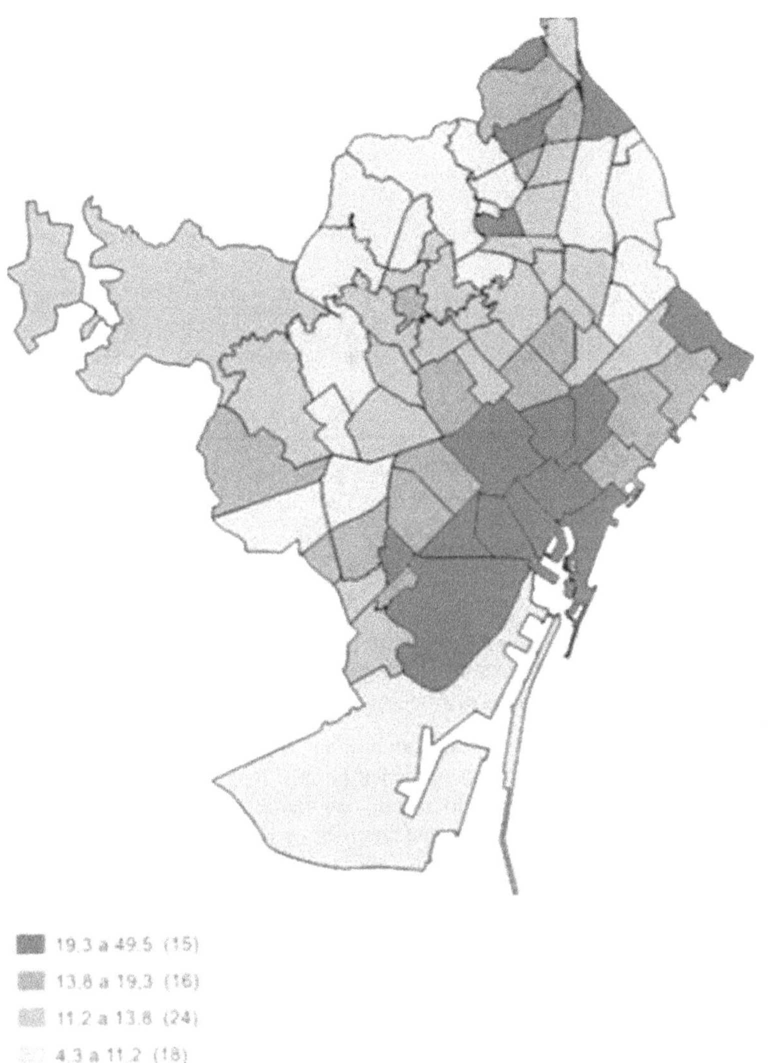

Source: Estadístiques de Barcelona.

Table 1.9. Distribution of foreign residents in Barcelona at the district level, 2015

Districts	%foreign /total population (main nationalities	Av. rent €/m2* per month
Barcelona	**16.6**	**11.1**
	(Italy, Pakistan, China)	
Ciutat Vella	43.2	12.4
	(Pakistan, Italy, Philippines)	
Eixample	18.7	11.2
	(Italy, China, France)	
Sants – Montjuic	18.7	10.7
	(Pakistan, Italy, China)	
Les Corts	11.2	12
	(Italy France, China)	
Sarria-Sant Gervasi	11.2	12.9
	(Italy, France, Germany)	
Gracia	15.9	11.8
	(Italy, France, China)	
Horta Guinardo	11.7	9.9
	(Italy, Bolivia, Morocco)	
Nou Barris	14.8	8.9
	(Honduras, Ecuador, Pakistan)	
Sant Andreu	11.4	9.6
	(China, Pakistan, Morocco)	
Sant Marti	15.4	10.6
	(Italy, China, Pakistan)	

Note: * Estimation of the average price for monthly rent, 2015
Source: Estadístiques de Barcelona; Ajuntament de Barcelona (2016c)

Notes

[1] In Spain, foreign residents can apply for the Spanish nationality after ten years. This general rule is flexible: it is reduced to five years for refugees and two years for residents born in Latin America, Philippines, Ecuadorian Guinea, Andorra and Portugal.

[2] (1) Through family reunification a migrant can reunite with his spouse, parents or children once they have renewed their initial work and residence permit. It is subject to being able to provide proof of sufficient economic resources to sustain the family and an appropriate home for the household, which must be confirmed by municipalities or regions through a specific report. (2) Residence and work permits are granted jointly and are conditioned by the national employment situation.

[3] In a strong industrial regional context: the industrial sector generates 19.6% of Catalonia's total Gross Value Added being the top region of the country in terms of industrial development and representing a quarter of the national industrial production (AMB, 2014; AB 2017a).

Chapter 2. Responses to migrant integration in Barcelona

This section is structured following the ***Checklist for public action to migrant integration at the local level, as included in the Synthesis Report*** (OECD, 2018) and comprises a list of 12 key evidence-based objectives that can be used by policy makers and practitioners in the development and implementation of migrant integration programmes, at local, regional, national and international levels. This checklist highlights for the first-time common messages and cross-cutting lessons learnt around policy frameworks, institutions, and mechanisms that feature in policies for migrant and refugee integration.

This innovative tool has been elaborated by the OECD as part of the larger study on *"Working Together for Local Integration of Migrants and Refugees"* supported by the European Commission, Directorate General for regional and urban policies. The Checklist is articulated according to four blocks and 12 objectives. This part describes the actions implemented in Barcelona following this framework.

Box 2.1. A checklist for public action to migrant integration at the local level

Block 1. Multi-level governance: Institutional and financial settings

Objective 1. Enhance effectiveness of migrant integration policy through improved vertical co-ordination and implementation at the relevant scale.

Objective 2. Seek policy coherence in addressing the multi-dimensional needs of, and opportunities for, migrants at the local level.

Objective 3. Ensure access to, and effective use of, financial resources that are adapted to local responsibilities for migrant integration.

Block 2. Time and space: Keys for migrants and host communities to live together

Objective 4. Design integration policies that take time into account throughout migrants' lifetimes and evolution of residency status.

Objective 5. Create spaces where interaction brings migrant and native-born communities closer.

Block 3. Local capacity for policy formulation and implementation

Objective 6. Build capacity and diversity in civil service, with a view to ensure access to mainstream services for migrants and newcomers.

Objective 7. Strengthen co-operation with non-state stakeholders, including through transparent and effective contracts.

Objective 8. Intensify the assessment of integration results for migrants and host communities and their use for evidence-based policies.

Block 4. Sectoral policies related to integration

Objective 9. Match migrant skills with economic and job opportunities.

Objective 10. Secure access to adequate housing.

Objective 11. Provide social welfare measures that are aligned with migrant inclusion.

Objective 12. Establish education responses to address segregation and provide equitable paths to professional growth.

Block 1: Multi-level governance: institutional and financial setting

Objective 1: Enhance effectiveness of migrant integration policy through improved vertical co-ordination and implementation at the relevant scale

An overview of the multi-level governance setting of Spain's highly-decentralised organisation

Spain is a decentralised country with three tiers of sub-national governments each of them responsible for specific competences determined in the Constitution and Statutes of Autonomy. In comparison to OECD countries sub-national government expenditure represents 20.8% of GDP (OECD average is 16.2%) and 49.2% of public expenditure (OECD average is 40.4%) (OECD, 2018b). Along with the national government (1) Autonomous Communities (CA), (2) Provinces and (3) Municipalities hold specific administrative competences as well as decision and management autonomy. The *Government delegations* are territorialised representations of the central government in autonomous regions and within them, the Government Sub-delegations are territorialised representations of the central government in provinces.

Understanding the general organisation of these various levels of government is essential to analyse the multi-level governance of migrant integration (See Figure 2.1). In such a complex institutional and regulatory landscape of shared competences, multilevel governance is essential to coordinate the wide array of highly interdependent actors and institutional structures at multiple levels. While the central government and its delegations manage migrant regulation, key integration domains are handled by subnational governments (See Annex B).

Figure 2.1. General scheme of the multi-layered government setting in Barcelona

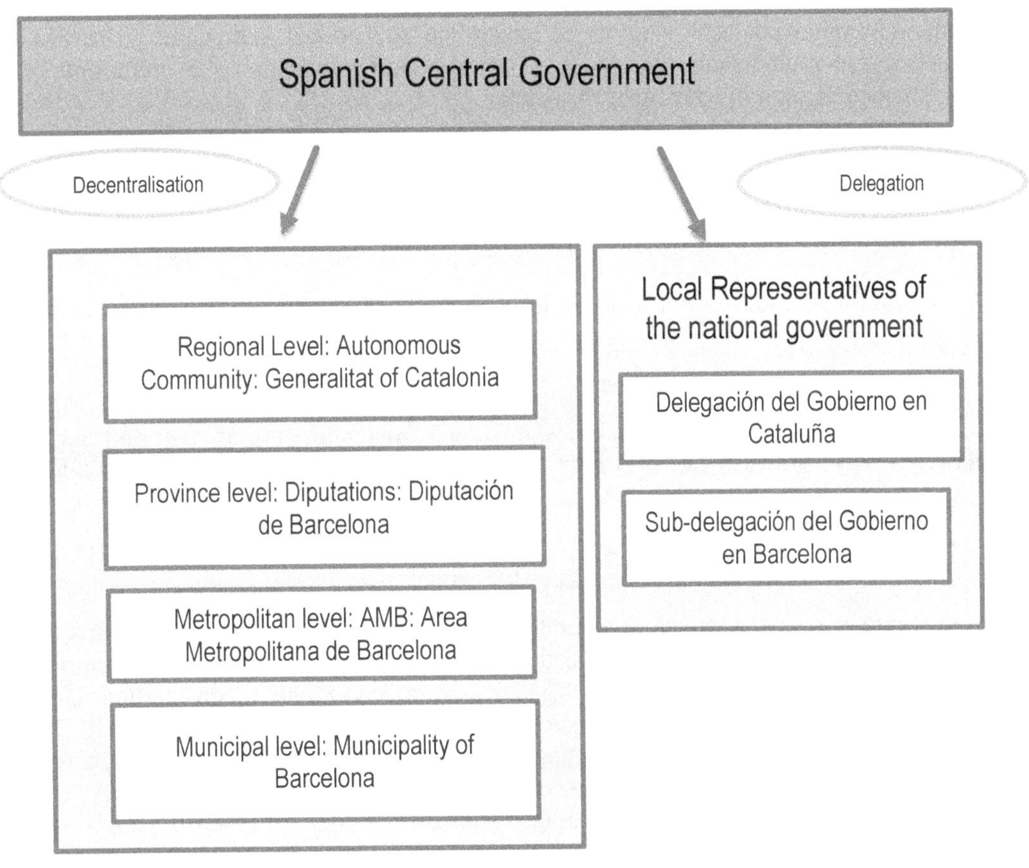

Source: Author's elaboration.

National level: approach and competences for migrant integration

National approach to migrant integration

As Spain was a country of emigration rather than immigration until the late 1990s, the definition of specific jurisdictional powers (see Chapter 1) and a correspondent approach and policy framework for migrant integration was not considered essential until then. In the meantime, subnational governments all over the country, which are closer to migrant integration realities and have key related competences, have taken the lead in the implementation of migrant integration programs. A similar situation has been observed in Vienna, Austria.

In Spain's short history of immigration, migrant regulation and integration has been approached through employment lenses and placed under the control of the Ministry of Employment and Social Security (MEySS). In 2007, the MEySS developed a National Migrant Integration Policy: National Strategic Plan for Citizenship and Integration or PEC (PEC 1: 2007-2010; PEC2: 2011-2014), thus defining the Spanish integration approach. Since sub-national governments have several competences for migrant integration and they have already set their plans to meet local needs, the PEC established a common framework and attempts to streamline subnational approaches. The PEC recognised the multidimensional scope of migrant integration and the promotion of coexistence in the new diverse Spanish society.

The 2009 reform of the LO 4/2000 stipulated the need for migrant integration polices and established that all public authorities shall promote the full integration of foreigners into Spanish society and that the public administration shall incorporate the goal of integration with a cross-cutting nature and there must be cooperation between levels of government

Competent stakeholders for migrant integration at the national level

Migration, nationality, asylum, border control and international relations are exclusive competences of the central government.

In Spain, unlike many European countries, it is the **Ministry of Employment and Social Security (MEySS)** which oversees both migration control (i.e. permits) and integration policy.

- Within the MEySS, the General Secretariat for Migration and Emigration (SGIE) designs and manages the procedures for residence and work permits.

- Further, the MEySS sub-directorate of Migrant Integration (SD-MI) designs the Strategic Plan for Citizenship and Integration (PEC) and manages the national migrant integration policy which receives European Funds for integration. Until 2011, under a subsidiary approach, the MEySS allocated funds (around EUR 200 million per year) to Autonomous Communities for migrant reception and integration. Since then, following budgetary constraints, the budget was suspended. The ministry allocates subsidies, through EU-AMIF funds and national funds, to non-governmental organisations for migrant integration through open calls for bids. The 2014-2020 National Programme for the Allocation of AMIF funds in Spain has three key objectives and its budget allocation reflects national priorities and observed trends: 1) Asylum which is managed by the MEySS and Ministry of Interior (28.74%); 2) Integration and Legal Migration (28.60%); 3) Return to country of origin (44.66%)[1]. Local Administrations do not receive EU-AMIF funding directly.

- The MEySS coordinates the social protection programme for asylum seekers (See Objective 3)

- The MEySS oversees the three coordination mechanisms for migrant integration at the national level (See Box 2.2).

- The MEySS holds other key competences for migrant integration as it designs the national employment policies and oversees the SEPE *(Servicio Publico de Empleo Estatal)* which is the national body allocating unemployment allowances to all residents with work permits. There are 12 SEPE offices in Barcelona.

The **Ministry of Interior** is responsible for border control as well as asylum. Further, the Interior Ministry manages the Centres of Internment of Foreigners (CIE) to which irregular migrants subject to possible expulsion can potentially be sent by a judge's decision according to the European Directive 2008/115.

The **Ministry of Justice** has exclusive responsibilities over naturalisation procedures to obtain Spanish nationality.

The **Ministry of Health and Social Services** establishes national guidelines in terms of health policy and distributes funding to Autonomous Communities (e.g. Generalitat of Catalonia), which manages the health system and designs territorialised polices including for non-Spanish people.

The **Foreign Office within the Sub-delegations of the central government in Barcelona,** which is the representation of the central government in the province of Barcelona, is the competent administration for migrant admission and receives applications for residence and work permits. Of high relevance is the permanent coordination between the Foreign Offices and the municipal *Secretariat of "Welcome policies for migrants"* to accompany migrants in their application processes and provide them with the right documents

---

Box 2.2. Coordination Mechanisms for Migrant integration at the national level

There are three formal coordination mechanisms for migrant integration at the national level in Spain.

1. The National Council for Social Integration of Migrants is coordinated by the MEySS (SD-MI) and takes stock of the wide array of stakeholders involved in migrant integration. This consultation and information sharing platform provides state-of-the-art migrant integration tools and is composed of (1) ten representatives of migrant associations; (2) ten representatives of social action NGOs; and (3) ten public administration representatives including six ministries, two representatives of Autonomous Communities and two representatives of Municipalities. The two municipal representatives are chosen through the federation of mayors, FEMP, which encompasses 90% of municipalities in Spain. Yet several municipalities in big Spanish cities, including Barcelona, are not currently represented in the FEMP and hence are not involved or benefit from this consultation and information sharing platform.

2. The Tripartite Social Committee, overseen by the MEySS, is a consultative forum through which trade unions, employers and national administrations periodically exchange information and have debates on migrant integration. A specific sub-committee on refugees has been established. This sub-committee is informed prior to the arrival of any resettled or relocated refugee. The Tripartite Social Committee shall be consulted prior to the approval of the labour market shortage list and any regulation related to migration. Subnational governments are not involved in this coordination committee.

3. The Inter-Ministerial Commission on Foreigners is a cross-sectoral mechanism that includes all ministerial departments with competences related to migration and asylum. All regulations that could affect migrant or refugees are supposed to be analysed by this committee.

Regional level: The Autonomous Community of Catalonia

Along with the national government, there are 17 Autonomous Communities with executive and legislative powers. The Autonomous Community of Catalonia is governed by the Generalitat of Catalonia. The competences and financing system of Autonomous Communities and their relationship with the central government, are asymmetric and defined in the Autonomy Statutes (the Catalonia Statute dates from 2006) and are inscribed in the framework of the Spanish Constitution.

The competences of the Autonomous Community (Generalitat of Catalonia) comprise health, education, social services, transport and communication, culture, local economic development, agriculture and energy, urban planning and civil protection. The Generalitat is also responsible for migrant integration (not asylum seekers) within the framework of its competences.

As several key sectors of the multi-dimensional character of migrant integration fall within the regional competences, the Generalitat launched Catalan Integration plans for migrants. The first Catalan Integration Plan was launched in 1993 and has been followed by five other integration plans during the 2000s, the last being the Citizenship and Migration Plan 2017-2020. The central idea of the plan is equality of rights and opportunities between foreign and Catalan residents, and access to mainstream services for migrants.

The **Department of Labour, Social Affairs and Families** oversees employment activation and social inclusion polices in Catalonia by managing:

- The Occupational Services of Catalonia (SOC) which design, implement and finance labour market orientation programmes, vocational training programmes and entrepreneurship workshops to which migrants with work permits have access.

- The General Secretariat of Migration of the Generalitat, which oversees migrant integration programs in Catalonia, has a budget that comes from both regional (Generalitat) funds and European Social Funds (FSE). This Generalitat Secretariat contributes 20% of its budget to the municipal reception mechanism Secretariat of Welcome policies for migrants of Barcelona; the rest is allocated to the remaining of the Catalan region. Also it provides, along with the municipality, the social inclusion reports required for the "Arraigo" procedure and the reports proving housing adequacy required for family reunification. For the provision of such reports, municipality and the Generalitat work in close coordination since in the city of Barcelona most of the reports are made by the municipality under the supervision of the Generalitat.

The **Department of Enterprise and Knowledge** can allocate initial work permits since the decentralisation reforms of the National Foreign law (see Chapter 1). They are granted jointly with the national government and conditioned by national employment situation.

The **Health Department** manages the health system and designs policies at the regional level according to national guidelines. The Department of Health of the Generalitat plans and designs the health policy of Catalonia and launched a compensatory programme to preserve the universal character of the health system

---

Box 2.3. A cross-sectoral programme at the regional level

The Health Department and the General Secretariat of Migration of the Generalitat worked together and co-implemented a specific programme for migrant female teenagers from Sub-Saharan countries. The programme aims at preventing genital mutilation after short visits into home countries by co-organising preventive sessions, a test before departures as well as a check-up upon return, which subjects the parents to six years of prison if upon return to Spain genital mutilation has been practiced. 160 teenagers in Catalonia followed this programme in 2016.

The municipality of Barcelona: its special regime and the use of "consortiums" as multi-level governance devices

The municipality of Barcelona, like Madrid, has a special regime. The 1998 chart of Barcelona defined the competences, the organisation of the municipality and its financial system. Larger competences were assigned to the local authority and some are under shared jurisdiction with the regional level. In Barcelona, municipal competences include urban planning, public transport, social services, education, health, social housing and culture.

The Barcelona municipality has a financial trajectory that is different than that of the country's average public administration. In 2016, the city had a budgetary surplus of EUR 97.5 million and 19.5% of gross savings reflecting both an historical strict financial strategy and a solid tax base. This contrasts with the overall deficit of Spain's Public Administrations (-4.3% of GDP), of the State (-2.7%) and Autonomous Communities (-0.8%; and the specific case of the Generalitat of Catalonia (-0.9%)). Local administrations had a surplus of 0.6%. In 2017, the municipal budget of Barcelona was EUR 2 739 million (See 2.1.3 for further details on municipal budget allocation).In the policy domains of shared responsibility with the Regional level, allocated due to its special regime, inter-governmental entities – the Consortiums – have been established.

Within the common education framework established at the national level, Autonomous Communities manage the education system. This includes primary, junior high and high school as well as adult education. The **Education Consortium,** directed by the Education Department of the Generalitat and the Social Rights Directorate of the municipality, designs and implements the educational polices of the city. The co-financing of this inter-governmental entity (60% by the Generalitat and 40% by the municipality), allows the local authority to have a greater impact in the educational programmes and to balance funding shortages.

The shared responsibility over housing by the Generalitat and the municipality is implemented through the **Housing Consortium.** This Consortium is co-managed by the Department of Governance, Public Administrations and Housing of the Generalitat (60%of financing) and the secretariat of Housing (within the directorate of Social Rights) of the Barcelona city council (40% of financing). The Housing Consortium regulates access to social housing in Barcelona. It manages *Bagur-SA,* which is a public municipal company financed with municipal capital. This is the entry point for all social housing users or demanders, including migrants. *BagurSA* also offers rent subsidies, legal assistance and manages the social housing stock. In 2017, the governance of housing in Barcelona changed. The municipality created the Municipal Institute of Housing and Rehabilitation (See Objective 2) which integrated *BagurSa* competences and actions.

Interaction with neighbouring municipalities to reach effective scale in social infrastructure and service delivery for migrants and refugees

Within each Autonomous Community there are provinces. In Catalonia, there are four provinces, one of them is the province of Barcelona. The provincial administration (*Diputación*) does not have competences in terms of migrant integration or implement policies pertaining to integration.

Acknowledging that the boundaries of the municipality of Barcelona did not fit with the broader functional urban area, the Barcelona Metropolitan Area (AMB) was created in 2011 uniting 36 neighbouring municipalities. The AMB is the administrative body of the metropolitan area and manages cross-sectional policies such as urban planning, mobility and transport as well as environmental protection. Its creation replaced three existing entities and streamlined the metropolitan governance of Barcelona. The mayor of Barcelona heads the AMB which includes 90 councillors representing member cities.

The AMB has no competences in terms of migration nor does it implement relevant policies and there is no partnership between metropolitan local authorities on this matter. Yet, further coordination with neighbouring municipalities could better address migrant integration at the right geographical scale and improve the quality and efficiency of services targeting migrants. Such a cooperative approach setup for joint service provision and resource sharing is implemented by the city of Gothenburg, for instance.

Objective 2: Seek policy coherence in addressing multi-dimensional migrant needs at the local level

At the national level, examples of a multi-sectoral approach toward migrant integration can be found in the platforms presented in Box 2.3.

City vision and approach to migrant integration

The city of Barcelona implements local integration policies following a specific integration strategy at the city level, which is set out in several strategic plans. Overall, the Barcelona approach to migrant integration could be summarised by three key principles: (1) Integral and fast reception for newcomers to foster integration from day one as well as a lifelong orientation; (2) equal access to rights and obligations as residents of the city and to multi-sectoral municipal services; (3) promotion of diversity and inter-culturalism as intrinsic to the city to preserve social cohesion. These principles are reflected in different municipal strategies and plans.

Since the late 1990s and the 2000s the municipality has implemented a strategy to enhance inter-culturalism. Taking stock of the existing migrant integration approaches implemented in neighbouring settings more experienced in receiving newcomers, and conscious of its respective benefits and difficulties, the municipality implemented municipal integration plans through an intercultural approach (Zapata, 2015). Based both on egalitarian values and principles of cultural freedom, intercultural policies promote tolerance, non-discrimination and highlight the need to create spaces for positive interaction, communication and intercultural relations among diversity (Alvarez Enriquez, 2013; Gimenez, 2003).

The local integration policies are guided by two sets of strategic plans: First, the municipal Working Plans on Immigration (2002, 2008-2011, 2012-2015) and a specific plan for reception mechanisms aim at achieving migrant integration at every level of civic life and identified immigration policies as cross-cutting to address the specific needs of newcomers while preserving social cohesion. The plans establish measures to (1) ensure rapid attention to newcomers when arriving, (2) pursue equity through a mainstreaming approach and lifelong orientation for migrants, (3) promote diversity and positive interaction as essential to preserving social cohesion. Second, the municipality developed two Intercultural Plans. A pioneer intercultural plan was launched in 1997 when foreign residents accounted for a mere 2% of the overall population to preserve foreigners' cultural diversity while enhancing their inclusion through a mainstreaming philosophy (Zapata, 2015). The 2009 plan was elaborated with the participation of the civil society, including migrant associations and social non-governmental entities. The central tenet is positive interaction and enhancing relationships among diverse citizens to curb social segregation and preserve social cohesion (AB, 2008; 2010; 2012).

More recently, the municipality launched the "Municipal measure to favour the access to regularisation and prevent irregularity" in order to improve reception and integration of people living in Barcelona in irregular situations (AB, 2017c). Protecting and supporting this specific public is a key priority of the current municipal council. More details about this element are in section 2.2.1.

City institutional setting with relevance to migrant integration

The city of Barcelona has an elected mayor and a city council. The municipality is currently organised in five "Areas" directed by Vice Mayors which are elected politicians. Each "Area" oversees different "commissioners" which coordinate "Secretariats". While there is a directorate of "Citizens rights, Participation and Transparency" with a Migration Commissioner and three secretariats specialised in migration, all the Municipal Migration Plans recognise the cross-cutting dimension of migration and other directorates are involved in migrant integration since they are responsible for key sectoral policies (i.e. housing, social services, education).

The Area of Citizen Rights, Participation and Transparency – Commissioner of Migration. The Area of Citizen Rights, Participation and Transparency has five commissioners one of them being the Migration commissioner who coordinates migrant integration at the municipal levels, actions which are undertaken by three secretariats in charge of specific areas. The role of the Migration commissioner is essential and effective to ensure policy coherence and collaboration between the three secretariats involved in migrant integration.

1. *The Secretariat of Welcome policies for Migrants* designs and implements the reception mechanism, information and the integrated support provided to migrants through the migration one-stop-shop (SAIER). A close partnership is engaged with local NGOs through contracts for long-term delegation of services. This secretariat also produces reports proving social inclusion for migrants who are trying to obtain residents permits through the "arraigo" procedure. It works hand-in-hand - and shares information - with the Generalitat and the *"Foreign Offices"* of the central Government sub-delegation. Further, the secretariat increasingly finances emergency shelters for migrants – even though this is not their competence (Social Rights and the Ministry of Employment and Social Security is responsible for emergency accommodations for asylum seekers).

2. The *Secretariat of Citizen rights and diversity* promotes coexistence in diversity, inter-culturalism and anti-discrimination, ensuring that longstanding communities are receptive and interact with newcomers. A permanent coordination is established with non-governmental actors with whom they co-design and co-implement intercultural programmes as well as literacy and Spanish language courses (See Objective 7 and 12).

3. *Barcelona Refugee City* was recently created to improve the existing mechanisms for asylum seekers and refugees in the city in a context of increased asylum in Europe. This municipal initiative was created in 2015 when the municipality declared that Barcelona was a "Refugee City". It provides all refugees arriving in Barcelona with the necessary services in the aim of providing a comprehensive and permanent refugee policy model at the local level. In collaboration with local NGO partners, a programme for asylum seekers and refugees was created in 2016 to complement the national programme: the Nausica programme, which includes temporary housing structures and an integral support structure for vulnerable asylum seekers and refugees (See page 55).

The Area of Social Rights manages social inclusion policies in the city including education, health, social services and housing. The measures implemented under this "Area" do not specifically target migrants yet this population benefits from them within the mainstream universal approach of access to municipal services. The end goal is to provide equal opportunities to all residents. Besides managing the municipal side of the Education and Housing Consortium mentioned above, two other fundamental domains for migrant integration fall under the competence of this "Area": social housing and social services.

1. The *municipal Housing Commissioner* designs housing policy in the city and directs the Municipal Housing Patronat (PMHB), a public company self-financed but managed by the municipality which builds, administers, buys and maintains the social housing stock of Barcelona. The Patronat generates its revenue from renting and selling housing units, credits from the private market, national subsidies for developing public housing and contributions from the municipality. The current municipality has made the 'right to housing' a key priority. Besides designing a new housing action plan, the city modified in 2017 the governance of housing at the local level with the creation of the Housing Municipal Institute (IMH). The IMH is overseen by the municipal housing Commissioner and centralises all housing-related services formerly implemented by the Municipal Housing Patronat and Bagursa including the promotion, management and allocation of social housing, support in housing rehabilitation, economic allowances for households unable to pay housing costs and detection of empty flats for their conversion into affordable housing. This governance reform aims at simplifying citizens' access to all housing services managed by the same entity.

2. The *Secretary of Social Action* oversees municipal social services and emergency attention in the city aiming to provide universal access and complementing the welfare benefits provided by the Generalitat. They manage temporary shelter and public facilities for homeless residents, mainstream social support and orientation for vulnerable residents but also grants for basic social services for emergency situations to which all people living in Barcelona are eligible regardless of their legal status. This Secretary works in close cooperation with the Secretariat of "Welcome policies for Migrants" sharing information and redirecting users. Access to these emergency grants is assessed by social workers (e.g. from the Social Services Centres – CSS) (See Objective 11).

The Area of Enterprise, Culture and Innovation. Although it does not have competences with regards to employment activation, the municipality created in 1986 the complementary agency *Barcelona Activa* to foster economic development and enhance employment and entrepreneurship to transform Barcelona into a knowledge city in a context of tense socio-economic climate, unemployment and economic restructuring (OECD, 2010b). Under the supervision of this Area, *Barcelona Activa* has developed several employment programmes including a start-up incubator, programmes for business support (e.g. access to finance), employment promotion workshops through the employment hub (Porta 22) like training programmes and matching between unemployed and private companies. Barcelona Activa is wholly-owned by the municipality but some programmes are financed by the Generalitat, the EU and the municipality while others just depend on the municipality. The latter are accessible to all residents regardless of legal status. The national government also works together with *Barcelona Activa* regarding visa and permits for entrepreneurs and highly-qualified migrants. *Barcelona*

Activa, working together with start-ups, identifies new employment needs or gaps and informs the national authorities.

The Area of Ecology, Urbanism and Mobility has exclusive responsibility for urban planning (increasingly shared with the metropolitan authority). There is an historic tradition of pubic investment in area-based urban policies in Barcelona targeting specific neighbourhoods for regeneration. Some examples can be found in Ciutat Vella (e.g. Rambla del Raval) or Nou Barris (i.e. Metro extension) which are districts with high presence of migrant population.

Further, the current municipality is highly engaged in reducing socio-economic inequalities within the city and has implemented a cross-cutting policy to bridge the divides between neighbourhoods (See Box 2.4).

Box 2.4. A cross-cutting place-based policy to bridge inequalities among Barcelona residents: The Plan of Neighbourhoods (Pla de Barris)

In 2016, the municipal council launched the Neighbourhood Plan to bridge inequalities through economic, social and urban measures by targeting the 16 most socio-economically impoverished neighbourhoods.

The targeted neighbourhoods were based on vulnerability indicators and an assessment of territorial inequalities (i.e. household's disposable income, socio-economic privation, housing, education, unemployment and health inequalities). The Neighbourhood plan is a cross-cutting programme that targets four key domains (education, social action, economic activity and urban renewal). It develops specific actions based on local challenges, needs and specificities. Some of the targeted neighbourhoods are also those in which foreign residents are over-represented (e.g. Ciutat Meridiana and Raval).

This central policy led by the current municipal council, is implemented in close collaboration with civil society and has received an extraordinary municipal budget of EUR 150 million on a ten-year horizon to bridge inequalities in the city. The 2017 budget was EUR 19.6 million and the 2018 budget proposal is for EUR 49.7 million. In 2017 Foment de Ciutat, a municipal company managed and coordinated the Neighbourhood Plan, which involves a complex governance structure including (1) all municipal Areas; (2) a wide set of social action NGOs and civil society initiatives that participate in the design and implementation of the Neighbourhood plan; (3) as well as external experts.

See http://pladebarris.barcelona/ca for more information.

Increasing formal coordination between the municipal areas on migrant integration would improve policy coherence and the pursued cross-cutting approach.

Figure 2.2 summarises the coordination mechanisms between levels of government on migrant and refugee integration.

Figure 2.2. Institutional mapping for migrant and asylum seeker integration

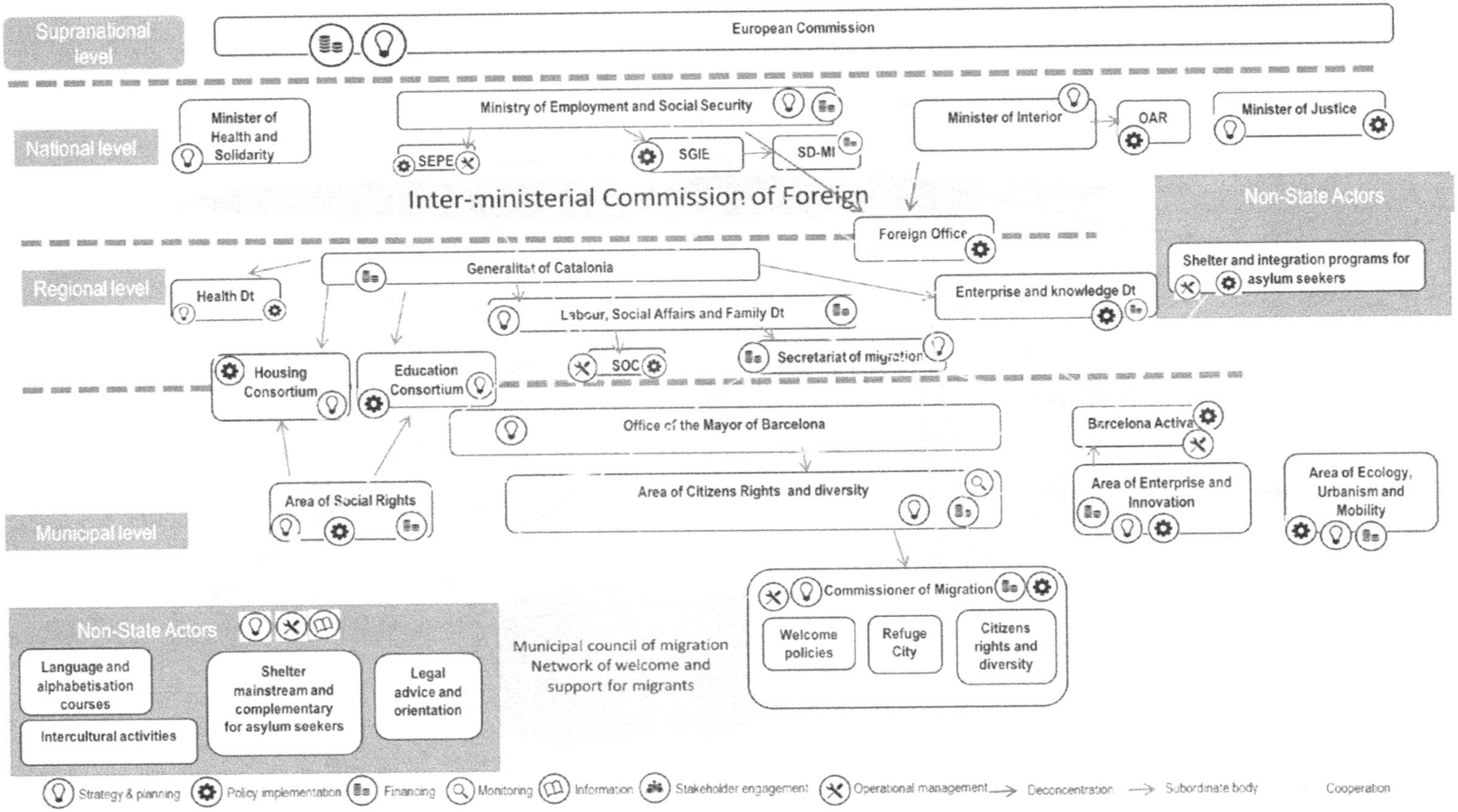

Source: Author's elaboration.

Objective 3: Ensure access to, and effective use of financial resources that are adapted to local responsibilities for migrant integration

At the national level, the Ministry of Employment and Social Security (MEySS) is the main actor managing funding for migrants' and asylum seekers' reception and integration. The ministry allocates over EUR 300 million for migrant integration and asylum seeker reception to non-governmental organisations to foster integration of migrants through open calls for bids (Source: Data provided by the MEySS). As the competent authority for accommodation facilities and the asylum integration programme, the MEySS also receives European funds (EUR 260 million allocated through the AMIF and ESF), which are directly managed by the MEySS or allocated to partner NGOs that manage the national accommodation facilities for asylum seekers. Until 2011, following a subsidiary approach, the MEySS allocated the funds assigned to the Strategic Plan for Citizenship and Integration (PEC), to Autonomous Communities (around EUR 200 million per year). As mentioned in 2.1.1, since then, following budgetary constraints, this budget has been eliminated.

In addition to their standard budget (from taxes and grants), the regional authority (Autonomous Communities) can receive European Social Funds (ESF) that can be used for migrant integration policies. Some 20% of the Generalitat's integration funds from the General Secretariat for Migrants are allocated to the Barcelona Secretariat for Welcome Policies for Migrants, which are mostly transferred from European Social Funds.

The municipal budget is EUR 2 739 million (2018) and its main sources are central government transfers and local taxes. In 2018, the main expenditures are in order of importance: (1) Housing and urban planning (EUR 455 million); (2) Urban services (EUR 356 million); (3) Social Services and social promotion (migrant reception and specific budget) (EUR 335 million); (4) Mobility and security; (5) Public Transport; (6) Culture; (7) Education; (8) Economic development and employment; (9) Environment; (10) Sports; (11) Health.[2]

The Migration Commissioner of the Municipality of Barcelona, which coordinates migrant integration programmes, handles an overall budget of EUR 15.7 million divided into three programmes: 1) Services to immigration and refugees (EUR 9.3 million); 2) Social promotion of immigration (EUR 3.4 million); 3) Human rights and non-discrimination (EUR 3 million). This budget includes EUR 1.2 million allocated by the Generalitat of Catolonia from European Social Funds. Since 2011, the municipality stopped receiving Spanish and European funding allocated to the central government (i.e. AMIF funds) which are instead now allocated to NGOs by the MEySS through open calls. The Commissioner extraordinarily provide stop-gap financing for emergency shelter (i.e. pensions and hostels nights) for migrants and asylum seekers (i.e. Phase 0), the cost of which increased by 47% between 2015 and 2016 and reached EUR 1.9 million in 2017. These extra funds were shifted away from other municipal budget items (See Objective 2) (Saier (2016) and municipal internal budgetary documents).

Addendum to Block 1: Multi-level governance of asylum seekers and refugee reception and integration mechanism

The asylum process step by step

The National Social protection programme for asylum seekers established a four-step programme for the social protection and integration of asylum seekers in Spain.

Phase 0: Evaluation and diagnostic of the application for asylum seeker status (While traditionally this phase lasts 1-2 months, recent increases in the number of arrivals have extended Phase 0 to 5-6 months (data in April 2018)

- Register in the Foreign Offices of the sub-delegations of the Government in Barcelona

- The Interior ministry (OAR) evaluates the application for asylum-seeker status

- Shelter provided to vulnerable applicants by the Ministry of Employment and Social Security (MEySS) within the National Social Protection programme for asylum seekers in collaboration with partner NGOs. In July 2017, an additional temporality criterion was added: can only be sheltered in this pre-phase applicants who have been in the national territory for less than 6 months and on European Union soil for less than two years. The municipality of Barcelona provides additional shelter in this phase to avoid increase in vulnerability and homelessness of applicants not filling the dual criteria, an increasing number since the July 2017 modification.

- If the application is recognised by the Interior Ministry (OAR) (a), the applicant becomes an asylum seeker and his or her international protection application will be analysed. Otherwise (b), the individual becomes a rejected asylum seeker required to leave the country or enters a phase of irregularity.

Phase 1: Reception (6 months) (Up to 9 months for vulnerable asylum seekers including pregnant women, single mothers, handicapped, unaccompanied minors)

- Once their application has been accepted, all asylum seekers are hosted in flats or communal hostels managed by partner NGOs or in centres directly managed by the MEySS

- Geographical mobility: location criteria based on availability of spots in the accommodation facilities in the national territory as well as features and characteristics of the families. A decision is made at the national level by the MEySS according to inputs provided by NGOs managing the accommodation facilities. There is no direct communication between the MEySS and local authorities on opening accommodation facilities for asylum seekers.

- Early integration measures are provided by the MEySS through delegation with NGOs. The integration measures include social, legal and psychological support, language learning, orientation towards education and the labour market.

- After 6 months the asylum seeker is entitled to work and obtains a residence permit

Phase 2: Integration (6 months) (up to 11 months for vulnerable asylum seekers)

- After the first six months the asylum seeker leaves the housing facilities. It is worth noting that in this phase asylum-seekers are highly mobile within the national territory and municipal authorities are not aware of the number and characteristics of asylum-seekers living in their locality.

- Provision of accommodation facilities is replaced by a monetary allowance for living expenses (to cover housing, food, transport, medication and education expenses) allocated by the central government based on a standardised national amount. The economic allowance depends on family composition and totals EUR 1,200 per month for a family of 4 people - a nationally standardised amount which is not tailored to local specificities. An essential issue in Barcelona is increasing housing costs which makes it difficult to access housing under the national standardised allowance.

- Phase 1 early integration measures are maintained: social, legal and psychological support, language learning, orientation towards education and the labour market.

Phase 3: Autonomy (6 months)

- Temporary economic and social support can be allocated by the MEySS

- The integration process is considered to be completed: asylum seekers are considered self-sufficient as they have at this stage obtained either refugee status or subsidiary protection.

Institutional setting for asylum and refugee integration in Spain and Barcelona

Art. 149 of the Spanish Constitution establishes that the central government has exclusive competence over asylum (as well as migration, nationality and border control). Art. 13 established the conditions under which asylum can be obtained and the 2009 Asylum law regulates international protection in Spain by establishing the categories of refuge and subsidiary protection (See page 55).

At the national level

In Spain, asylum procedures and integration of asylum-seeker integration are exclusive national competences regulated by the central government under shared responsibility of both the Interior Ministry (asylum legal procedure) and the Employment and Social Security Ministry (integration programme for asylum seekers).

The Ministry of Interior oversees the asylum procedure through the Office of Asylum and Refugee (OAR) once registered in the Foreign Offices of the subnational delegations. First, the OAR evaluates the application for asylum made at the Foreign offices and either recognises or not the person as an asylum-seeker. This process traditionally lasted between one and two months, yet recent increases in arrivals are causing delays in the registration of asylum procedures. In 2017, the average waiting time for an appointment to register asylum applications was six months (CEAR, 2018). In April 2018, the Interior Ministry increased its capacities to address the increase in applicants and hired more public workers to diagnose and evaluate the applications for asylum-seeker status. During this phase of evaluation and diagnosis of the asylum application, vulnerable applicants have access to shelter (Phase 0 of the National Programme for Asylum Seekers implemented by the MEySS). If the OAR recognises the application, the person becomes an asylum-seeker and the asylum procedure starts. The recognised asylum-seeker has access to the protection programme for asylum seekers coordinated by the MEySS and implemented with partner NGOs, which includes accommodation facilities and an integration programme (Phase 1, 2, 3). In 2015 in Spain, there were 15 887 asylum applications and the numbers doubled in 2017 with 31 563 asylum seeker applications. Out of the 13 350 decisions taken in 2017 (which do not refer to the 2017 applications since the average asylum procedure lasts 14.4 months), 65% were negative (8675) and 35% were positive (4675), which is a recognition rate that is 10 percentage points below the European average. Among the 4 675 individuals receiving international protection in Spain, 4 080 received subsidiary protection and 595 refugee status in 2017 (Eurostat, CEAR, 2018; ACCEM-ECRE, 2017).

The Ministry of Employment and Social Security (MEySS) through the SD-MI designs and oversees the National Social Protection Programme for asylum seekers, which includes accommodation facilities and the integration programme and is financed with national and European funds (AMIF) (See page 80). Through AMIF and ESF, EUR 260 million were allocated by the EU 2014-2020 for refugee and asylum seeker integration to Spain. The MEySS works in close coordination with two stakeholders. They include the OAR (Ministry of Interior) with whom they share information on the progress of the asylum procedures and NGOs that are contracted through "*Convenios*", i.e. long-term delegation of service agreements, to implement the programme across Spain. These NGOs provide early integration measures and manage most of the housing structures in which asylum seekers are initially hosted. Until 2012, there were three partner national NGOs (The Red Cross, Comissión Española de Ayuda al Refugiado (CEAR), Accem). In response to the increase in asylum seekers, the MEySS has bolstered the national capacities addressing asylum-seeker integration by expanding the list of partner NGOs to 20 (ACCEM-ECRE, 2017). In Barcelona, five NGOs are under contracted and manage the national accommodation facilities for asylum seekers: Comissión Catalana d'Ajuda al Refugiat (CCAR), Accem, Cruz Roja, Apip-Acam, Bayt-Al-Taqafa and Cepaim. The selection of NGOs was based on experience on asylum, adhesion to the programme philosophy and diversified presence in the national territory. There is no communication between the national government and local authorities on the opening of accommodation facilities at the local level.

At the local level

The local impact of the national programme for asylum seekers is substantial. Along with increased asylum applications in Barcelona, which have risen in the last years (Figure 1.3), the city attracts a great deal of asylum seekers because of the metropolitan labour pool and existing migrant communities, once the National Programme allows migrants to circulate freely across Spain (Phase 2). Until 2018, there is no evidence of information sharing or coordination between the national government and the local authority with regards to asylum seekers and refugees.

While asylum and refuge issues are exclusively national competences, the municipality of Barcelona has always supported asylum seekers and refugees by responding to their local needs. Reacting to the increase in asylum seeker arrivals in the city, the municipality adapted its traditional mechanisms as other European cities have done.

In particular, the municipality responded to the needs of specific migrants who are not covered by the national asylum programme including four main categories : (1) those whose protection status has not been decided yet after the 18 month of duration of the national protection programme or who have been recognised but are not yet autonomous (i.e. didn't find a job or an accommodation, etc.; (2) individuals whose application for asylum is under evaluation (i.e. Phase 0) but who do not meet the "vulnerability" or "temporality" criteria required to be sheltered before being recognised as asylum seekers; (3) asylum seekers having declined the national programme not accepting the required geographical mobility; (4) asylum seekers in phase 2 of the national programme who are unable to afford the cost of living in Barcelona with the standardised allowance allocated by the national social protection programme.

Traditionally, the municipality has supported asylum seekers through the Secretariat for Welcome Policies for migrants and its collaboration with the Red Cross, which is one of the NGOs working within the municipal migration hub (SAIER). The Red Cross is also one of the MEySS's partner NGOs and manages the National system of attention and integration of asylum seekers in Barcelona. The municipality provides the SAIER space and logistics as well as translation services and complements shelter needs. The sharp increase in asylum seekers has squeezed SAIER capacities. In 2012, 304 individuals required attention and information about asylum in the SAIER, this number swelled to 2,292 in 2016. Out of the asylum seekers attending the Barcelona migration hub (SAIER), 23% are homeless. The SAIER and regular municipal social services finance temporary shelter to asylum seekers fitting in the categories mentioned above: in 2016, the municipality financed emergency shelter to asylum seekers with a municipal cost of EUR 320 000. In 2017, the municipality allocated one-off funds of EUR 1.9 million to shelter migrant and asylum seekers. According to budgetary documents provided by the municipality, the migration Commissioner spent EUR 207 506 for the month of October 2017 in shelter for migrants (spending half of this amount on asylum seekers fitting the categories mentioned above). In the month of March 2018, it reached EUR 312 171. The municipal services believe that this emergency response is pressuring the capacities of the municipal migrant integration services and crowding out regular municipal social services such as municipal shelters (See Objective 3 and Objective 11).

Since 2015, through the municipal Refuge City team, the municipality launched the *Nausica* programme for asylum seekers and refugees. This complementary municipal structure offers integration attention to asylum seekers who are not in the national programme (i.e. the four categories above). This structure is developed in close coordination between specialised NGOs, some of them already implementing the national programme and other local non-profit social entities specialised in asylum. Nausica includes six months temporary housing in flats owned by the municipality and managed by the NGOs, an integrated individual support (professional, legal, medical and social support, education orientation, language learning and cultural activities) as well as covering for living expenses during the length of the programme. Nausica is completely financed by the municipality with a budget of EUR 1 135 098 between 2016 and 2017 (EUR 293 173 in 2016 and EUR 949 277 in 2017). A set of standards prioritise vulnerable applicants (e.g. families, pregnancy, victims of violence and discrimination, illness, elderly, etc.). Collaboration with experienced partner NGOs allowed the municipality to be aware of the specific needs of LGTBI asylum seekers, and the local government set aside one of the accommodation facilities for such individuals.

Further multi-level dialogue, information sharing and coordination on domains as accommodation facilities and integration programmes for asylum seekers and refugees, could improve the outcomes of the policies implemented in terms of efficiency and quality of the service, enhancing integration and social cohesion.

Block 2: Time and Space: keys for migrants and host communities to live together

This section aims to describe the leading principles along which reception and integration policies are designed at city level. Across the cities analysed in the study "Territorial Approach to migrant integration" of which this case study is part, the concepts of time and space appear to be essential in implementing durable integration solutions. Time refers to the life-long process of establishing oneself in a city, and the need for solutions to be provided along this process. Besides the objective of facilitating the integration of newcomers, cities must offer entry points for foreign-born or even native-born individuals with a migrant background, to facilitate development throughout their lives. Space is understood as proximity and is well illustrated by the concept of "Connecting" that many cities have adopted in their approach to integration. This concept acknowledges that inclusion does not result automatically from living in the same city but requires real interaction. Cities have a role to play in encouraging such interaction, by supporting local level initiatives and creating public spaces, where connections among different groups can spark a dialogue and all components of the society (host communities, long standing migrant communities, business, etc.) can play their role in a multi-directional integration process.

Objective 4: Design integration policies that take time into account throughout migrants' lifetimes and status evolution

It is increasingly evident that migrant integration requires public action over time and the Barcelona municipality has taken stock of this essential component in its integration strategies. A central component of Barcelona's approach to migrant integration is the comprehensive welcome system that starts right after arrival and remains accessible throughout a migrant's lifetime. Acknowledging that migrant integration is a long process, the municipality tries to involve migrants through an advisory body to improve long-term integration.

An integrated welcome system for newcomers in Barcelona

The Service Centre for Immigrants, Emigrants and Refugees (SAIER), created in 1989, is a one-stop-shop for migrants in Barcelona. All categories of migrants, regardless of their legal status, find information and counselling, in several languages, about in- and out-migration, asylum, refugee and voluntary return at the offices located in the city centre. It is an integrated municipal service, funded with municipal and regional funds. The SAIER is accessible regardless of legal status[3]. This specialised migration hub is jointly managed by the Secretariat of Welcome Policies for Migrants of the city council and partner private stakeholders (NGOs, trade unions and specialised labour organisations), which have offices within the SAIER (See Objective 7; See Box 2.5)

The main role of the SAIER is to inform and support residents about migration and integration topics. It is composed of three areas. First, a front desk, where basic questions are answered in 12 different languages. There is also a general information service and specialised services managed by partner stakeholders (See Box 2.5). The specialised SAIER services provide support on matters such as language learning, legal advice, health, labour research and skills-recognition and about the national programme for asylum and refugees. The SAIER can also re-direct the users to public or non-state entities such as migrant or neighbourhood associations that complement this support.

A key role of the SAIER for migrant integration is its continued support throughout the application for permits and its production of the required "Arraigo" reports justifying the integration efforts for participants of SAIER activities. The SAIER and the Foreign Offices of the sub-delegation of the central government in Barcelona closely collaborate improving coordination for the regularisation procedures.

Further, the SAIER provides social assistance to the most vulnerable users referring them to the municipal Social Services or directly providing emergency assistance. This includes information but also financing basic sustenance and emergency shelter when needed for the most vulnerable migrants such as undocumented migrants and asylum seekers to avoid homelessness and social exclusion (SAIER, 2016). As mentioned, according to SAIER (2016), emergency shelter expenditure increased by 47% between 2015 and 2016, (from EUR 549 445 to EUR 809 945) evidencing the high pressure of housing costs for migrants in Barcelona.

Complementary to the SAIER, Service of Orientation and Support for Migrant People (SOAPI) are territorialised municipal offices to welcome and support migrants at the district level. SOAPIs are found in the 10 offices of the municipality at the district level. SOAPIs provide information and support to migrants about migration procedures, access to public services (particularly the health system), rights and obligations and about the cultural and social life in the city.

New Families: A specific mechanism for the reception of reunified families

Following an increase in family reunification applications, the municipality created the New Families programme. In 2016, more than 2 000 families benefited from it.

The rationale behind the programme is that family reunification has the potential to contribute substantially to migrant integration. It reflects a long-term commitment of the newcomer to the host society, can favour his personal sociocultural stability and balances the gender distribution of certain migrant communities. This positive effect is not spontaneous and requires policy action to maximise the beneficial contribution of families. The municipality created the service to support migrants before, during and after family reunification. The programme provides a three-step support for families through the process of arrival of the reunified members – either parents, children or spouses.

Table 2.1. The New Families programme for family reunification support

Before the Family Reunification procedure	Once application for Family Reunification accepted	After arrival of the reunified family
Legal and administrative advice to apply for family reunification	Psychological support for parents to prepare the arrival after long-term separation with family members. Also, guidance through the administrative procedure.	Support at the household level to accompany the family and ease their integration in the city. Also, specialised workshops for parents, women and teenagers.

The municipality supports both legally and psychologically migrants in Barcelona before and after reunification. After reunification, the support remains and is complemented with specialised workshops for vulnerable or potentially-isolated incoming members of the family such as teenagers and women. The women workshops aim at preventing isolation. Statistics on participants of the project show that only 7% of the women are working or looking for a job, and 70% have not legalised their education degrees since their purpose is to reunify with their husbands. The workshops consist of language and cultural classes to help reunified migrant women be more autonomous in the city and ease their socialisation. Teenagers can benefit from accompaniment during their integration in the school system as school dropout rates are high among reunified youth. An evaluation of the programme showed that participating teenagers integrated smoothly in the school system (CIIMU, 2013).

The inclusive approach to the local administrative census as an instrument for integration

The national law establishes the existence of an administrative municipal census – the *Padron* – in which every person living in Spain must be registered, automatically gaining the status of "neighbour" of the municipality. The Padron is managed by the local authority and is not shared with other administrations unless required for the exercise of their competence. All newcomers can register in the Padron regardless of their legal status they only need an identification document– either national or foreign – and a residence address in the municipality. The Padron does not give the right to legally reside in Spain. Local authorities can adopt different positions towards this register and the public facilities accessible through it.

The city of Barcelona, has made the decision to adopt an inclusive view towards the Padron. This inclusive approach, which is also adopted by some other Spanish cities, is an essential decision for migrant integration, which materialises in two ways. First, the municipality allows those without a permanent address to register with a temporary one. Second, through the *Padron* registry, regardless of legal status, Barcelona residents not only have access to education, as foreseen by national law, but to almost all municipal services of the city. This approach towards the *Padron* provides newcomers with services from day one, avoiding extreme vulnerability while waiting for regularisation, and provides the municipality with detailed information on all its inhabitants reducing informality.

A municipal action to protect irregular migrants in the city

Along with the historic inclusive use of the Padron, the current municipal council is highly engaged in protecting irregular migrants' integration in Barcelona (Spencer, 2017).

Since legal entrance in Spain is conditioned on national labour, family reunification or humanitarian reasons and very few visas are given for labour purposes in the current economic context, many migrants currently enter the country with touristic visas or irregularly. Often, they remain undocumented for a period of three years before being able to obtain work and residence permits through the "arraigo" procedure. During this period, migrants work in the informal sector and cannot access national and regional public services (e.g. employment, social housing and welfare facilities). Further, rejected asylum-seekers and people whose permits have lapsed also enter in phases of irregularity (See page 29).

In 2017, the Barcelona City Council designed and adopted a unique and comprehensive Action Plan to curb risks of social exclusion of irregular migrants, diminishing the impacts of irregularity on their long-term integration perspectives (AB, 2017d)[4].

The Action Plan addresses negative consequences of migrants' irregular situation, which affects integration, including (1) the development of an informal job market in which worker's rights are more easily exploited especially in the domestic and care economy, tourism and construction sectors; (2) immigrant workers' exposure to economic cycles and hence job instability, which affects their wages and job conditions and destabilises general labour conditions; (3) distrust of access to public authorities and fear of interment or deportation; (4) administrative exclusion from national and regional services (e.g. employment, welfare and public housing services are inaccessible); (5) heightened risk of social exclusion and segregation linked to irregularity.

The Action plan, which is currently in its implementation phase, has five objectives and provides a set of concrete actions, an implementation timetable and budget to improve the municipal action towards irregular migrants. These include guaranteeing access to municipal services for irregular migrants including language learning facilities or increased information and legal support for irregular migrants. Specific attention is given to economic sectors with more irregular migrants and precarious labour conditions such as domestic and care work. Close collaboration with *Barcelona Activa,* the employment agency of the city, allowed for the development of specific labour market integration programmes for irregular migrants. First, it makes access to the municipally-financed vocational training programmes of *Barcelona Activa* (See Objective 9) universal. Further, a specific municipal budget is allocated to 12-month employment programmes for irregular migrants including vocational training and work placement experiences aiming to facilitate regularisation through the "arraigo" procedure.

A consultative mechanism: The Municipal Council of Migration

The Barcelona migration working plan 2012-2016 acknowledged the need to enable migrants to be active citizens with participatory capacities to organise political proposals (AB, 2012).

Barcelona has a vast network of NGOs and neighbourhood associations as well as migrant associations specialises in various aspects of migrant integration, based on their nationality (by locality, country or continent of origin) and demographics (Women, LGTBI, Youth, etc.) (See Objective 7).

Since 1997, Barcelona has a local consultative body, the Municipal Council of Migration (CMIB) to encourage migrants' presence in the local political sphere and to be informed of their position in the policy-making process on integration matters. It is seconded by the Municipality and chaired by the Municipal Commissioner of Migration and a representative of a migrant association. Representatives of migrant associations jointly produced - with the municipality - a working plan with strategic goals for the 2019 horizon and suggested initiatives to achieve them. They included increased inter-culturalism, promotion and support of migrant associations and improved internal organisation of the CMIB. This platform is key to collect information on the pressing issues affecting migrant communities in the city. The CMIB also allows representatives from diverse migrant associations and backgrounds to meet and interact. Through this platform, non-governmental stakeholders share information, communicate and coordinate their work.

A pending topic is the one of representation, political rights, and access to decision-making bodies. Individuals who do not have Spanish national are forbidden by the Constitution to vote in local elections, which is not the case for other civic duties and benefits. Only foreign residents from countries having signed reciprocity agreements can vote in municipal elections, which excludes *de facto* most migrants, notably Asian and African migrants.

Objective 5: Create spaces where interaction brings migrant and native-born communities closer

Finding opportunities to bridge the divides and foster togetherness between migrants and natives is a key concern and the municipality addresses it along with civil society organisations. Inter-culturalism and the promotion of mutual knowledge and positive interaction among diverse residents are at the heart of the concept of migrant integration in Barcelona. Along with the design and implementation of anti-discrimination policies, the facilitation of intercultural relations and meeting spaces is a strategy to enhance migrant integration and preserve present and future social cohesion at the local level. The secretariat of "Citizen's rights and diversity" is in charge of these policies. In 2017, the municipality considered that - while the 2000s were a period of intensification of arrivals in which the reception mechanisms needed to be adapted - a current issue to address for migrant integration is also discrimination and promoting interaction among diverse residents.

The Anti-rumours programme

The "anti-rumours programme" intends to build a counter-narrative to rumours about migrants dispelling the myths towards foreigners and constructing a positive discourse about diversity. The municipality organises awareness and communication campaigns (e.g. booklets and comics) to stop the misperceptions about foreigners, showing evidence, refuting fake rumours and giving counter-arguments. The municipality also organises capacity-building workshops to enable witnesses of discriminatory attitudes towards foreigners to intervene. In its six years of existence, up to 3 000 anti-rumour individual agents have been trained in Barcelona (including public administration staff, members of non-governmental associations, private companies and individual citizens) An inner-city network of more than 400 NGOs has been trained and subsidised to develop anti-rumour initiatives to improve communication about migration. Following the terrorist attacks that hit Barcelona on 17 August 2017, the programme ramped up their communication and awareness rising on the topic in an effort to curb the increase in rumours and discriminatory messages on social media targeting ethnic and religious affiliations.

Anchored in an intercultural perspective, the municipality launched in 2017 a Plan to Combat Islamophobia with the goal to portray Islamophobia as a form of discrimination, counteract the spread of negative images about Islam, normalise religious diversity and reinforce mechanisms against this form of discrimination. This 18-month plan has a budget of EUR 55 000 and has been designed with the participation of academics, anti-racism NGOs, Muslim organisations and residents, including youth and women. The municipality decided to intervene against Islamophobia as a phenomenon of stereotypical speech and discrimination towards Muslim residents (or those perceived as such). The plan consists of a set of measures in the short term (e.g. awareness campaigns, inclusion of Islamophobia as a form of discrimination in the directive of the Municipal Police), middle term (e.g. school workshops on stereotypical views of Islam and religious diversity, support for Muslim organisations in creating the "Day Against Islamophobia") and long-term measures (e.g. establish an observatory for hate crimes, guide for municipal workers, etc.).

Supporting inter-culturalism at the neighbourhood level

The local authority subsidies civil society associations active at neighbourhood level (which include NGOs, migrant and neighbourhood organisations) to undertake intercultural projects and communicate through an intercultural lens. An example of this is the Festival "Soups of the World" organised by several organisations in Nou Barris, a district on the outskirts of Barcelona that has historically been a hub for both domestic and international migrants. This initiative, in which neighbours from all over the world cook soups from their own culture, symbolises the benefits of a co-existence in diversity and of positive interaction. Various neighbours interact during the cooking process and share food, thus fostering mutual knowledge and triggering confidence between newcomers and long-standing communities.

The network of neighbourhood public libraries is also a key tool for municipal promotion of intercultural relations. These public facilities are also situated in disadvantaged neighbourhoods and promoted as spaces of positive interaction among diverse residents. For example, the public library in Ciutat Meridiana built in 2009 improved the quality of public spaces in one of the poorest neighbourhoods on the outskirts of the city with a very high migrant concentration. The library has books in several languages and has targeted the activities offered to the needs of the neighbourhood. For instance, at the request of Moroccan women they activated IT classes for women only, which in turn attracted more women from both migrant and native-born backgrounds. After-school courses are open to kids of the neighbourhood and specific activities are organised for seniors (cinema club, reading clubs).

Involvement of native communities and interaction is a central factor for integration. In Barcelona, the municipality fostered the interaction among newcomer and long-standing shop-keepers. Since the mid-2000s, there has been an increase in ethnic retail shops in specific areas of the city (Serra Del Pozo, 2006). Acknowledging that the interaction between migrant shop-keepers and their Spanish peers was not spontaneous, the municipality coordinated events and programmes in cooperation with various stakeholders (e.g. NGOs, business associations, migrant and neighbourhood associations) to facilitate interaction. Such interactions are essential to foster mutual knowledge and trigger confidence at the neighbourhood level. An example of this was the forum "Retail and social cohesion" organised in 2007 and, more recently, the project XEIX in l'Eixample district which was awarded a 2015 Council of Europe distinction. XEIX was implemented in close collaboration between the municipality and Chinese and Spanish business associations to promote integration through retail-oriented activities including the creation of a commercial association for Chinese shop-owners, the organisation of events, and the organisation of common workshops to counteract stereotypes.

To physically portray the benefits of inter-culturalism and communicate about the diverse character of Barcelona, the municipality also created an intercultural centre: Espai Avinyó. The centre hosts cultural events such as exhibitions, concerts, conferences and several meetings about the diverse cultures of the city.

Block 3: Capacity for policy formulation and implementation

Objective 6: Build up capacity and diversity of public service, particularly in the key services of receiving migrants and newcomers

When accessing public services, newcomers can experience language and cultural barriers. Local civil servants' lack of knowledge and awareness of diversity and migrants' specific questions might also prevent newcomers from accessing the right services.

To address this issue, the municipality of Barcelona has provided the front-line service of the SAIER - one-stop-shop for migrants – with professionals managing 12 different languages and a system of phone-translators for other languages.

Beyond this frontline specific service for migrants, through the anti-rumours programme, the municipality organises capacity-building workshops and training for public administration staff, partner stakeholders and members of the civil society giving them tools to intervene when witnessing discrimination and prejudice towards foreigners. In six years of existence, around 3 000 anti-rumour individual agents have been trained in Barcelona. More recently, in March 2018, the municipality launched a new programme to curb racism and stop discriminatory procedures among municipal police forces.

In terms of representativeness it can also be noted that the First Deputy Mayor of the local administration is a migrant himself, which may improve the image of image as well as migrants' and citizens' expectations.

Lastly, the municipality participated in June 2017 in the Open Society Fellowship offered to a refugee based in Barcelona who has demonstrated commitment with his or her community. The recipient will work directly with the municipality on projects and programmes related to the inclusion of refugees and migrants. It increases the positive image of diversity and improves communication and collaboration between refugee and migrant communities and city policy makers.

Objective 7: Strengthen co-operation with non-state stakeholders, including through transparent and effective contracts

Civil society in Barcelona has traditionally been engaged in several social and political spheres. A vast network of non-profit initiatives and associations work in close collaboration with the local authority in several domains. Migrant integration has become one of the dimensions of their engagement.

There are three key categories of NGOs working alongside the public authorities in this area:

1. Non-governmental organisations (NGOs) specialised in different topics, public or neighbourhoods related to migration, asylum or to relevant topics for migrant, asylum seeker and refugee reception and integration

2. A diverse set of migrant associations created by newcomers and targeting migrants by origin, gender, age or sectoral domains;

3. Neighbourhood associations which have been highly active in the city. While not directly involved in migrant integration, they play a key role in fostering proximity and mutual knowledge between native and migrant communities working in close coordination with other associations, co-organising events and workshops at the neighbourhood level.

The municipality of Barcelona developed two consultation devices with non-governmental organisations which are essential coordination platforms (See Box 2.5) In Barcelona, like in other cities of the sample, NGOs and civil society initiatives are essential in bolstering and bringing municipal action to fruition. The municipality outsources the delivery of some public services to NGOs: it expands service availability, including to irregular migrants when they are ineligible for public services, and they relay migrants' demands to the local authorities. In Barcelona, their role is particularly important in implementing polices related to legal advice, labour market orientation and cultural activities. They are also active in offering Spanish learning and literacy courses (subsidised by the municipality). They are also pivotal in providing shelter as the limited social housing stock is restricted to regular migrants and the price tensions in the private rental sector highly affect low-income migrants (See Objective 10).

Box 2.5. Consultative platforms in the city of Barcelona for migrant integration

Barcelona has two coordination platforms enhancing information sharing and cooperation between NGOs, migrant associations and the municipality.

(1) The Municipal Council of Migration (CMIB) is a consultative local body were non-governmental actors involved in migrant integration can exchange and channel their demands to local representatives. The CMIB has an action plan – currently the 2016-2019 Work Plan – designed alongside the CMIB's member organisations and the institution itself and incorporates a projected timetable. In this plan, the goals and initiatives to achieve them are specified. The main thrust of the plan is:

1. The achievement of full citizenship as the CMIB published 67 proposals for the improvement of migrants' position in legislation

2. Inter-culturalism

3. The promotion and support of migrant associations

4. Internal running of the council

(2) Since 2007, the Network of Welcome and Support for migrants gathers the municipality and non-state actors (e.g. neighbourhood and migrant associations as well as social non-profit organisations) for coordination as well as material and methodological sharing on topics related to migrant integration. These actors are crucial in complementing the municipal programme for migrants' autonomous development in the city through language courses, legal advice, employment orientation, social support and cultural activities. The city backs their efforts with subsidies and by facilitating co-ordination among them within this network. Some examples of common actions produced through this network include the joint production of language learning material and integration guides or the organisation of events and journeys related to migration.

These partner stakeholders operate within three financial frameworks. First, they can be entirely privately financed as is the case of religious foundations providing shelter. Second, some of them have signed bi- or tri-annual contracts with the municipality. This is the case for partner private organisations providing essential services in the municipal one-stop-shop SAIER (See Box 2.6). Last, most non-governmental actors involved in migrant integration work through temporary subsidies allocated by the different government levels through calls for projects. This method was reported as causing financing and sustainability issues by partner stakeholders in OECD meetings. It was considered an unstable financial method as subsidies are granted annually – whereas projects for migrant integration last longer – but also because they are usually disbursed at the end of the year, which means that NGOs need to foot the bill upfront through private market loans. In addition, since subsidies can only finance up to 50% of a project, NGOs need to cumulate subsidies, which requires a capacity that they might not always have.

Box 2.6. Municipality and NGOs working together in delivering migrant integration services at the local migration hub SAIER

The SAIER is the municipal migration one-stop-shop in the city of Barcelona (See page 60) where municipal workers and partner NGOs deliver specialised services for migrants. Since SAIER's launch in 1989, key services have been outsourced to NGOs to gain efficiency as they were already experienced service deliverers in specific integration related domains. The SAIER is jointly managed by the Secretariat of Welcome Policies for Migrants of the city council and private stakeholders (NGOs, trade unions and specialised labour organisations) that share offices with the SAIER. The municipality renews contracts every three years with these partner stakeholders. In fact, out of 62 workers of the SAIER, the coordinator is the only public servant, the other workers are outsourced.

Table 2.2. Services provided at the SAIER by partner non-governmental stakeholders

Service provided (Name of the partner stakeholder)	Organisation	Number of users in 2015
Service reception and general information and support	NGO(ABD)	9 996
Social Attention and health	NGO (Red Cross)	1 563
Council and document processing	Trade Union(CITE)	4 122
Legal advice	Lawyers professional organisation(ICAB)	2 050
Legal advice for refugees	NGO(ACSAR)	699
Standardisation and recognition of titles and competences, Employment orientation	Trade Union(AMIC)	1 431
Language learning	Public entity(CNL)	1 074

Objective 8: Intensify the assessment of integration results for migrants and host communities and their use in policy design

An annual monitoring of foreign residents in Barcelona through the Padron registry

The existence of the local Padron registry allows officials to track, on an annual basis, foreign presence at the city, district and neighbourhood level and make comparisons at the regional and national scale. Through the Padrón, the municipality gathers information about migrants' nationalities, demographic profile, territorial distribution within the city and educational level. With this data and other statistical sources, the municipality's department of Statistics publishes an annual report on the foreign population in the city, which enables it to better monitor migration trends and outcomes and assess policy design for migrant integration.

Evaluate the performance of the migration one-stop-shop

The local one-stop-shop for migrants (SAIER) has the capacity to store data about its users, and to exploit and adapt its services accordingly. The SAIER produces an annual report about its users' demographic and socio-economic characteristics. As a result, the SAIER rapidly reflects migration trends and adapts its services to the needs of users. As an example, in 2013, the office started to provide information about emigration and voluntary return. More recently, to respond to the specific needs of asylum seekers and refugees, the SAIER recruited a supplementary psychologist on top of the two provided by the Red Cross. The information about SAIER users is also shared with the social services of the city (Area of Social Rights). This statistical monitoring is complemented by an evaluation of the service through focus groups and satisfaction surveys completed by its users. This includes an evaluation of SAIER staff. In 2016, 55% of SAIER users stated that the service was very good and 34% that the service was good (SAIER; 2016).

Track residents' perception and social values

The municipality monitors its residents' perception and social values through the Municipal Social Value Survey (MSVS). The MSVS, which is based on 1 500 personal interviews and published every four years, includes questions on several domains (e.g. taxes, migration, civic behaviour, etc.) and reflects residents' values over time. In particular, it illustrated the effects of the economic crisis.

Results from the 2014 Municipal Social Value survey indicated that Barcelona is a progressive city. Equality is considered as one of the most important values by 68% of residents (after freedom) and 80% consider that the State is obliged to provide decent living conditions for everyone (AB, 2014). Residents are favourable to diversity: in 2014 83% considered that it is better for a country if its residents come from diverse traditions and coexist with one another (AB, 2014).

The Municipal Social Value Survey includes the perception of residents towards migration among the topics monitored. Even in poor economic times and international migration flows, Barcelona residents have been welcoming and there has not been major conflicts. Any misgivings about migration have not been reflected in a political response (Zapata, 2015).

This generally positive perception of migration is not equally shared by all population groups as unemployed residents with low socioeconomic profile and the elderly tend to see migration with more reticence than the average (AB, 2014). Such perception is in conformity with statistical evidence about European regions provided by the OECD in the synthesis report related to the territorial approach to migrant integration (OECD, 2018).

Further, for over twenty years, the municipality has tracked residents' perceptions by undertaking, twice a year, an opinion survey called the "Barometer". The percentage of citizens who consider migration a problem has decreased in the past ten years even as the socio-economic context soured (See Figure 2.3). The comprehensive municipal policy to combat misconceptions and rumours about migrants might have contributed to this result (See page 64). The overall welcoming culture was also highlighted by a Mixities report (2013) and demonstrated in February 2017 when the civil society organised a walk to welcome refugees.

Figure 2.3. Changes in residents who consider migration problematic, Barcelona

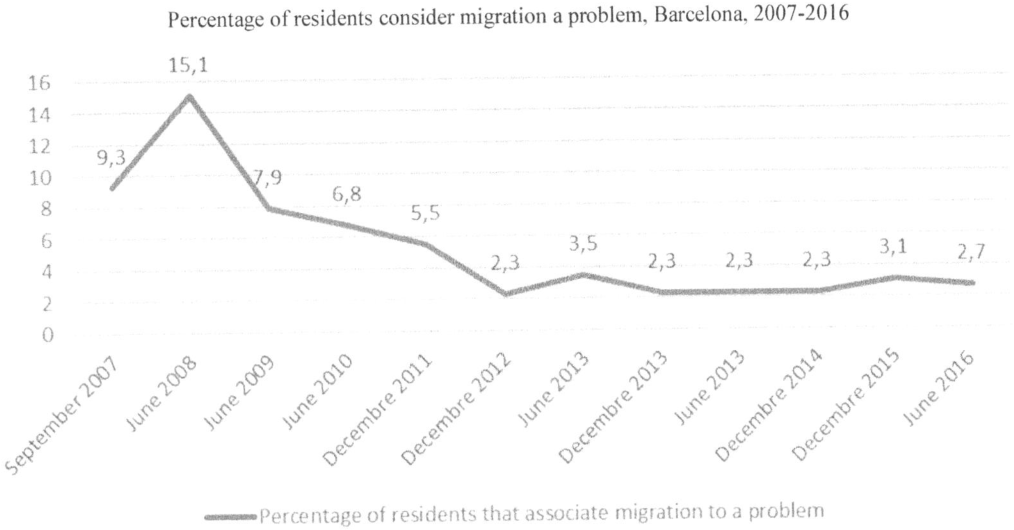

Percentage of residents consider migration a problem, Barcelona, 2007-2016

Source: Data provided by the municipality based on the Municipal Baramotre data. http://ajuntament.barcelona.cat/premsa/wp-content/uploads/2018/01/r17010_Baròmetre_Desembre_Evolució.pdf

Block 4: Sectoral measures for migrant integration

Objective 9: Match migrant skills with economic and job opportunities

Why is it important?

Employment is an essential aspect of the integration process. It is not only migrants' primary source of income but also a key entry to social integration by, for instance, supporting their access to adequate housing and facilitating their interaction with native born residents.

The Spanish labour market is highly affected by unemployment. The country ranks at the bottom half of OECD countries with an unemployment rate of 16.6% in 2017. During the economic crisis unemployment peaked (See page 32) particularly affecting foreign-born people. At the national level, the unemployment rate of non-EU foreign residents is 10 percentage points higher than the one of natives. At the level of the Catalonia Autonomous Community, where unemployment rate is lower than the country's average (14,9%), non-EU foreign unemployment is still much higher than the average (almost 30% in 2016) (See Table 2.3).

Table 2.3. Unemployment by nationality at the national and regional (tl2) level, 2016 T4

Unemployment rate by nationality, 2016T4		
	Spain	Catalonia
Spanish	17.8	13.1
Foreign: total	24.7	25
Foreign: EU	20.1	13.2
Foreign: Non-EU	27.4	29.2
Total	18.6	14.9

Source: Ministerio de Empleo y Seguridad Social.

National data on unemployment also indicates a three-percentage point gap between foreign-born men and women, the same proportion as the native-born gender gap (OECD data base on migration)

Local migrant unemployment reflects similar trends. One out of five unemployed is foreign in Barcelona.

Table 2.4. Changes in foreign unemployment as a percentage of total unemployed

Rate of foreign among unemployed				
	Barcelona (city)	Barcelona (province)	Catalonia	Spain
2011T4	22.1	20.6	22.9	14.2
2013T4	19.3	17.5	19.7	11.9
2015T4	17.7	16.9	19.9	11.9
2017 T4	19.7	17.7	20.7	12.2

Source: Barcelona Economia, Observatori d'Empresa I Ocupació and Ministry of Employment and Social Security.

A recent IERMB study (2017) shows that between 2005 and 2016, foreign unemployment rates almost permanently doubled Spanish rates in the province of Barcelona (See Figure 2.4). While with the economic crisis unemployment raised on both sides, the increase for foreigners is higher. In 2013, unemployment among foreigners reached 41.8% while for Spanish nationals it peaked at 20.9%. While economic recovery decreased relative unemployment, differences persist: unemployment for foreigners is double that of native Spaniards (IERMB, 2018; See Figure 2.4). In Barcelona, non-EU migrants largely work in wholesale and retail, tourism, construction and personal care, which are sectors with high levels of informality, low productivity and high exposure to economic cycles and downturns.

Figure 2.4. Unemployment rate by nationality, Province of Barcelona (TL3), 2005-2016

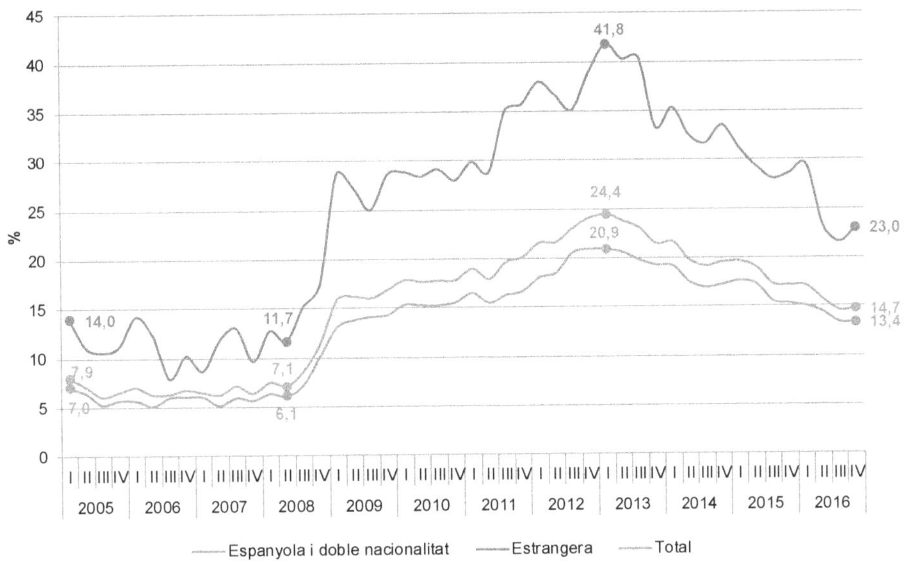

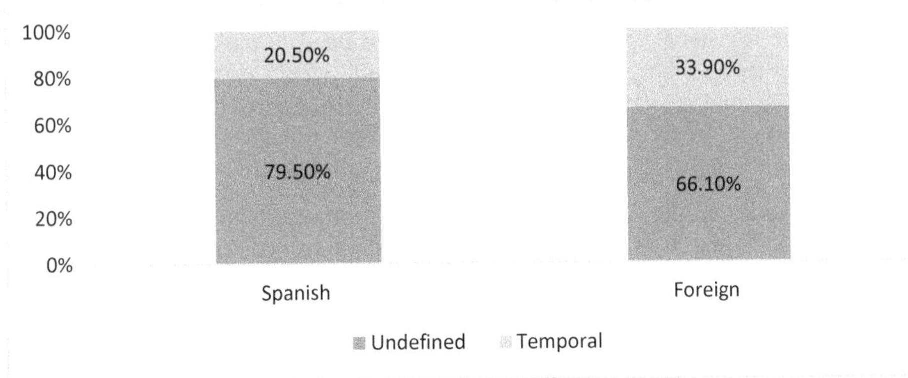

Note: Blue line - Spanish and double nationality; Orange line - Foreign nationality; Grey line - total
Source: IERMB (2017; 2018) based on microdata from EPA, INE.

Another essential element with which to assess migrant labour market integration is their over-representation among temporary contracts. While there has been an improvement of employment performance since the 2012 Spanish labour market reform, the labour market is increasingly dual and the labour market insecure. Since 2010, temporary contracts have increased by 10% while undefined contracts have decreased by 3.2% in Barcelona. Today, the breakdown between long-term and temporary contacts is 77%/23%, a dual structure which hurts migrants in particular (34% of foreigners work under temporary contracts, (AB, 2017c) (See Figure 2.5). Foreigners are thus affected to a considerable degree by low-quality, temporary contracts and thus more vulnerable to economic downturns (AB, 2017c; IERMB, 2018).

Figure 2.5. Employment by type of contract and nationality, Barcelona, 2015

Source: AB (2017c); Based on data from Mostra Continua de Vides Laborals (MCVL).

Often self-employment/entrepreneurship is a way into the labour market for migrants. Specific migrant communities are highly entrepreneurial in Barcelona mainly in the retail sector as is the case of Pakistan and Chinese nationals (Serra del Pozo, 2006; Guell, 2017). Their location is highly concentrated in the Ciutat Vella districts and correlated to the residential location of similar foreign groups (Serra del Pozo, 2006; Guell, 2017).

Local responses for migrant integration in the labour market

Provided they have legal authorisation to work in Spain, economic migrants and refugees benefit from full access to the labour market and are entitled to receive the economic integration services provided in the city by the different levels of government. The right to work and recognition of competences are national competences and do not depend on the local authority; however, the municipality plays a role as intermediary between migrants and local businesses.

While access to employment is not a municipal competence, the municipality has historically engaged in developing employment and local development programmes.

Local responses for migrant integration in the labour market are developed below. Traditionally, and adapted to a context of general high unemployment, Barcelona has not focused on developing specific policies for migrant labour integration but has actively promoted their integration in undifferentiated labour market channels addressed to the unemployed and vulnerable citizens of the city. Further, recently the municipality developed employment programs for undocumented migrants (See Objective 4).

Support for accessing the labour market in the migration hub

In the migration one-stop-shop (SAIER) through the outsourcing to the partner trade union- UGT-AMIC migrants are accompanied in their labour market integration. On site, UGT-AMIC provides support for diploma recognition, employment search and vocational training. These services are offered not only to newcomers but also long-standing migrants in employment difficulties, as has increasingly been the case after the economic crisis. The most usual profiles requiring support for labour research are ex-workers of the construction sector highly affected by the crisis or women working in domestic care services (SAIER, 2016).

Access to mainstream employment services

Migrants with work permits have access to the same employment activation programmes as nationals once registered as being unemployed (no need to have previously worked: e.g. recent graduates looking for a job with a valid work permit can enrol in the employment programs). In Barcelona, such schemes are offered both by the regional government –through the Occupation Offices of the Generalitat – and the municipality – through *Barcelona Activa*.

Migrants with work permits can register and benefit from the labour market orientation programmes, vocational training and entrepreneurship workshops developed by the Occupation Offices.

Barcelona Activa (See Objective 2) does not offer unemployment allowances but rather services including job hunting support, labour mediation, advice and training for self-employment and entrepreneurship-related services geared to specific sectors, vocational training, business incubators and business lending services. The local agency is financed mainly with municipal and European funds. Some 35% of Barcelona Activa's users are foreign from non-EU countries. More specifically, 24% of the users of the entrepreneurship programmes are foreign from non-EU countries; 34% of the users of the Labour Integration Programme addressed to people at risk of exclusion are foreign from non–EU countries. The latter is a programme addressed to unemployed residents at risk of exclusion or experiencing social difficulties. It consists in formulating a personalised path to access the labour market with individual tutoring, employment advice, skill development and pairing migrants with companies. It can be accessed through municipal social services. Foreign women use these services less (only 19% of the women using the entrepreneurship programme are foreign) and foreigners use less vocational training (e.g. only 7% of the participants in such courses are non-EU nationals).

The recent "2016-2020 Employment Strategy for Barcelona" included "attention to diversity" among its top priorities to "fight against the discrimination of groups such as LGTBI, immigrants, the disabled or those suffering mental health issues". With a EUR 15 million uniquely municipal budget, these programmes partially tackle migrant integration in the labour market since they are in part geared towards irregular migrants working in particularly vulnerable informal jobs. They include activities linked to the feminisation of poverty and the increased vulnerability of specific professional domains in which female migrants are overrepresented like domestic work.

Collaboration with the private sector for vulnerable residents' integration in the labour market

In 2016, the municipality Directorate for Social Rights launched an innovative programme to enhance access to employment for the most vulnerable unemployed residents of the city through training and direct partnership with private companies. *Labora* is a mainstream programme to which vulnerable residents of the city can have access (including migrants with work permits filling vulnerability criteria). Through a close coordination between the municipal social services, 2 000 private companies and NGOs, the programme Labora connects residents at risk of exclusion with private employers with matching and vocational training. The companies are ensured that the matched worker corresponds to its needs and receives support in the selection process. In addition, they benefit from incentives. First, it represents strong engagement with corporate social responsibility and the municipality delivers a "Labora seal" crediting the company as a "solidarity organisation". Further, participating companies can benefit from economic incentives from the Area of Enterprise and Employment of the municipality (i.e. up to EUR 12 000 allocated by person hired). In 2016, Labora had more than 8 000 participants and 1 967 contracts were signed in diverse sectors such as human care, retail and hospitality with partners companies including local branches of large European companies.

Working with the Social Economy to foster migrants' integration in the labour market

The municipality has also coordinated the creation of cooperatives within the social solidarity economy in sectors where irregular migrants worked in vulnerable positions such as street vendors or scrap-dealers. Becoming a member of the cooperative, the person can easily obtain regular status through a working permit, and improve their socio-economic situation and integration in the city.

Supporting private initiatives of the social economy has also been implemented by the municipality to foster labour market integration. *Mescladis* is an example of such a social enterprise for migrant integration. Through the programme Cooking Opportunities, Meslcadis offers vocational training to migrants as cooks and waiters according to their cultural and culinary skills to empower them in accessing the labour market. The training programmes last three months (around 250 hours of class) and around 70 migrants are trained every year. Mescladis has a restaurant where participants in the Cooking Opportunities programme practice and which partially sustains the programme economically.

Objective 10: Secure access to adequate housing

Access to decent housing as a bottleneck for integration

Access to good quality and proper housing is an essential aspect of migrants' well-being and successful integration. Poor-quality and unstable housing conditions tend to be associated with lower educational attainment, higher risks of social exclusion and poorer health status (Salvi del Pero et al., 2016).

Housing regulation is a national responsibility and the provision of public housing is generally under the competence of Autonomous Communities along with a municipal responsibility in the case of Barcelona. Historically, Spanish housing policy has promoted home ownership through fiscal incentives and social housing is marginal all over the national territory. In the city of Barcelona, public housing only accounts for a mere 1.5% of the housing stock (11 544 flats).

In this context of historical weak social housing availability, access to housing and spatial distribution of migrants is linked to housing access and affordability in the private rental market. The private rental market is the predominant channel for migrants' housing provision (Pareja-Eastaway, 2009), which renders migrants more exposed to price tensions in the private market. As mentioned above, if housing costs were not an issue only 19% of foreigners would be threatened by poverty in Barcelona, the part of them at risk of poverty, instead of the current 30% (See Table 1.8). There are major price tensions in the private rental market in Barcelona. International attractiveness is squeezing the private rental sector: between 2016 and 2017, according to the INCASOl, rental prices increased 11.4% on average in the city.

The preponderance of the rental sector and more empty and easy to rent flats through informal submarkets, smaller apartments and better affordability of the housing stock has turned historical downtowns into "welcoming districts" and long-term residence (Pareja-Eastaway, 2009) for foreigners. In fact, such housing is close to employment opportunities in the service sector and provide "agglomeration effects" – i.e. the support network and potential housing opportunities provided by previous cohorts of immigrants (Pareja-Eastaway, 2009; Castles, 2004). Traditionally, and unlike other cities where migrants only concentrated on the outskirts of the urban areas, the historical downtown of Barcelona (Ciutat Vella) has played a central function in housing migrants (See page 32).

Among the characteristics that help understand Ciutat Vella's traditional role as a gateway for migrants are (AB, 2015):

1. The part of the private rental market in this neighbourhood represent 56.5% of total housing stock, almost double than in the rest of the city where private rental represents 30% of the housing stock

2. living conditions are worse: 22% of flats have good accessibility versus 49% in Barcelona, and 30% are in bad or unsatisfactory shape (vs. 6% in Barcelona on average)

3. units are smaller (over 50% of the flats are under 60m^2);

4. the housing structure is very old (77% of the units were built before 1940 whereas in Barcelona only 11.4% of the stock was built before 1940)

Further, migrants have increasingly concentrated on the outskirts of the city in neighbourhoods such as Ciutat Meridiana, which was built in the 1960s to accommodate internal mobility inflows of workers from other parts of the national territory. Ciutat Meridiana was highly affected by the wave of foreclosures after the economic crisis and was nicknamed "Foreclosed city" *("Villa Desahaucio")* (Darribau and Bhandar, 2016).[5] Many foreign low-skilled workers having bought flats through mortgages in this area were among those with a high risk of arrears and defaults and over-represented among households experiencing foreclosures (Cano Fuentes et al., 2013). Further, the deepen price tension in Ciutat Vella, is increasingly triggering more migrants to leave the historical downtown. According to the INCASOL, rental market prices increased by 11.4% between 2016 and 2017 in Ciutat Vella, two percentage points above the city average, and have increased by 16% since 2013 in Ciutat Vella.

Overall in Barcelona migrant residents tend to live in more disadvantaged residential conditions marked by abusive rental conditions and overcrowding (Bayona and Rubiales, 2015). Some 30% of SAIER (2016) users declare having moisture, isolation or temperature problems in their homes and the neighbourhoods with more overcrowding in Barcelona are also the ones with more foreign residents (El Raval with 437 flats with more than 9 residents vs. 190 for the second densest neighbourhood).

Local policies for housing in Barcelona

Housing policy (i.e. rent legislation, social housing) is regulated at the national level. Social housing is implemented through a shared responsibility between the municipality and the region by the housing Consortium and the Municipal Housing Institute (formerly *BagurSa* and *Patronat de l'Habitatge*) which defines access to social housing, offers rent subsidies, legal assistance and manages the social housing stock. There is no specific policy for migrants' access to housing in Barcelona, which seems in line with a general context of housing shortages.

As mentioned above (See Objective 10), social housing is marginal in Barcelona and accounts for a mere 1.5% of the housing stock. Public housing is homogenously well distributed within the city being highly superior in Ciutat Vella (5%) and Nou Barris (3.5%) yet limited in comparison with other European cities (e.g. 20% in Paris). Migrants with permits having lived in the city for over a year can access public housing under the same conditions. In fact, 19% of public housing residents are foreign, and there is a high proportion of foreigners among renters of social flats according to data provided by the municipality. Building new public housing is difficult in Barcelona as natural barriers limit the city's expansion and there is almost no suitable land available.

The current municipal government has made housing affordability a strong priority. Housing and urban planning is the biggest expenditure of the municipal budget in 2018 (EUR 455 523 199). The municipality launched a 10-year 'Right to Housing Action Plan' *(Pla pel dret a l'habitage 2016-2025)*[6] with a set of objectives and actions to respond to the key local housing challenges identified in the city including increasing rent prices, evictions, lack of public housing or the use of housing units for touristic functions. The new municipal approach aims at guaranteeing the social use of housing. Among the actions pursued are buying empty flats from private banks or individuals to increase the stock of public and affordable housing as well as the prevention and support to residents at risk of evictions. Diagnosis and specific measures are designed according to different district needs. The overall budget of the plan supposes a total cost of EUR 2 973.2 million including EUR 1 666.2 million financed directly by the municipality.

Further, as public housing is limited, the municipality recently designed through the 2017 Neighbourhood Plan, "Anti-gentrification" clauses to protect affordable housing in central areas after regeneration processes. The municipality allocated subsidies for building rehabilitation and refurbishment in Ciutat Vella, but conditions it to an engagement of not increasing rent prices once the building improvements are complete.

Objective 11: Provide social welfare measures that are aligned with migrant inclusion

Social services and welfare measures

Previous sections have shown that there is a large gap between foreign and native-born income and employment levels meaning that migrants are potentially over-represented among social welfare users.

Social assistance in Barcelona

The provision of municipal social assistance in Barcelona follows a mainstream and universal approach and is accessible to all residents registered in the municipal Padron regardless of their legal status based on vulnerability criteria.

The municipality has a network of Social Services Centres (CSS) at the neighbourhood level that provide information, and advisory services to residents in socio-economic need. CSS are managed by the Secretariat of Social Action of the city, which designs, implements and finances the municipal social and emergency services. Among the functions of the CSS are the evaluation of needs, information and counselling to vulnerable residents, management of emergency welfare allowances and support in filling out administrative documents, referring specific cases to the specialised welfare and social services and to partner with social action stakeholders.

Along with the CSS, the municipal Area of Social Rights also manages the *Centre d'Urgències i D'Emergències Socials de Barcelona* (CUESB), which is a centre for social emergencies that offers continuous psychosocial services. The CUESB provides emergency services to vulnerable residents of the city who unable to cover immediate and vital needs (e.g. food, clothes, hygiene, health). The CUESB also provides temporary accommodation on-site or redirects individuals to hostels for stays lasting from 3 to 5 days. Once the emergency solved, the person in need is redirected towards the mainstream social service system (CSS) or specific specialised services (housing, health, etc.).

The municipality is responsible for providing basic social protection and for covering vital needs through social restaurants offering daily meals, as well as hygiene services (showering and changing clothes).

Provision of welfare allowances

Migrants with resident permits have access to the same welfare benefits as Spanish residents. The Generalitat provides a basic income (the RMI Renta Minima de Insercion, whose amount is fixed since 2011 at EUR 424/month) along with an individualised support plan (PI) for those in Catalonia in socio-economic difficulty whose own resources are not enough to maintain a decent standard of living. The RMI aims at supporting its beneficiaries with basic needs and preparing them for social and employment integration. Within the Generalitat, the business and Occupation Department finances the allowances and the Social Welfare and family department manages the RMI (control and follow-up). Receiving the RMI is subject to a list of conditions among which lack of income, housing vulnerability and children in the household as well as risk of isolation. Requirements include being "empadronado" –registered in the padron- of any Catalonian municipality, being a resident for a continuous time of two years and for foreigners to have a valid permit of stay. The standard amount is complemented for additional children, isolation or single-parent families. It has been observed that migrants do not make full use of this service, as they are often unaware of their entitlement. Only 23.8 % of Barcelona residents receiving the RMI are foreign which is below the rate of poverty of this group. To curb this trend, the municipality is engaged in raising awareness and providing information to migrants on this benefit through the SAIER.

Complementing the RMI, the municipal Area of Social Rights, provides basic additional funding thanks to municipal revenues to the most vulnerable categories of the population enrolled in the Padron regardless of legal status. As it is ultimately responsible for providing basic social services, the municipality finances - through the CSS - small emergency grants to vulnerable residents who need to pay basic bills in a variety of areas (rent, water, electricity, food etc.). The Secretariat of Welcome Policies for Migrants works in close coordination with the Area of Social Rights, sharing information and referring migrants to social services.

Health

Spain performs well in terms of health status comparing to other OECD countries (OECD, How is life in Spain). The allocation of competences is tripartite in the health dimension. The central government has the legislative competence on the basic regulation of the health system at the national level to ensure territorial coherence and, accordingly, the Spanish Ministry of Health establishes the general health guidelines. Health is under the jurisdiction of regional governments, which manage hospitals. The municipal level has few responsibilities in terms of health. Because of Barcelona's special regime, the city is co-responsible for Primary care health centres (CAP) as well as some hospitals.

In terms of access to healthcare, Catalonia grants universal access to the public health system to migrants regardless of their legal status based on a public health approach.

The role of the municipality in terms of access to health is limited to informing newcomers through municipal staff within the SOAPI and the SAIER to ensure that their right to access the healthcare system is upheld. The municipality also prints flyers in several languages including maps which are distributed through municipal social services to explain how to access the healthcare system. Further, Barcelona finances intercultural mediators to work with certain migrant nationalities affected by specific health problems.

Objective 12: Establish education responses to address segregation and provide equitable paths to professional growth

Why is it important?

While most adult migrants receive their initial education in their country of origin, the host country can play a significant role in enhancing migrants' educational level and qualifications to match the requirements of its labour market. Likewise, migrant child integration in the school system is essential and schools are usually the first point of contact between migrant families and the host society.

Adults level of education

The average qualification of Barcelona's residents indicates that foreign residents are on average better qualified since there is a lower illiteracy rate and a higher percentage of individuals holding university degrees. Yet, there are in fact two different trends among foreigners in Barcelona: most EU foreigners are highly qualified whereas non-EU residents tend to have few qualifications albeit to a lesser extent for Latin American nationals versus Asian or African residents (See Table 2.5).

Table 2.5 Level of education by nationality, Barcelona, 2011

Level of education (%)	Spanish	Total Foreign	Italy	Pakistan	Morocco	Bolivia
No studies	7.5	2.1	0	0.9	1.3	0.1
Primary	11.7	22.7	3.4	64.7	52.4	27.1
Junior High	20.8	18.1	9	20.6	20.8	29.1
High school and professional path	28.1	21.1	27.8	6	14.6	27.7
High professional path/ University	32	36	59.3	5.4	9.1	13.6
No information			0.5	2.4	1.9	2.4

Source: Ajuntament de Barcelona, Departament de Estadistiques; AB (2016a).

School outcomes and segregation of migrant children

Almost all foreign children of school age registered in the Padron are enrolled in the Catalan school system – with a small percentage enrolled in private international schools. While 60% of Spanish pupils are enrolled in private or semi-private schools, only 30% of foreign pupils are enrolled in such schools in Barcelona (CEB, 2016).

The distribution of foreign pupils across Barcelona's public schools reflects a spatial segregation: pupils with more difficulties are concentrated in public schools located in low-income neighbourhoods (IIAB, 2017). The IIAB (2017) notes that the uneven distribution of socially-disadvantaged pupils negatively impacts the latter in terms of school results as they have worse grades than the socially-mixed school centres. Foreign pupils are overrepresented in specific territories and schools - while 40% of Ciutat Vella pupils are foreign (55% in public schools), they represent 3.3% in the district of Sarrià Sant Gervasi, which are those with more schools considered of *"maximum complexity"* (in the districts of Ciutat Vella, Nou Barris and Sants-Montjuic) (IIAB,2017).

Foreign pupils are highly concentrated in the most disadvantaged schools, which negatively impact both their results and educational paths. In Catalonia, foreign pupils tend to score 10 points below native students (Generalitat de Catalunya, 2014 based on OECD PISA results 2012). In Barcelona, the rate of foreign pupils who have to repeat grades is higher, especially for boys. In Ciutat Vella, the neighbourhood with the most foreign pupils, 6.3% of 16-year-old Spanish boys repeat grades (which is higher than the city's average) versus 19.2% of foreign boys (IIAB, 2017) (See Table 2.6).

Table 2.6. Percentage of students repeating grades by gender and nationality in the last year of Junior High (4t ESO), 2015-2016, Barcelona

	Girl Spanish	Girl Foreign	Boy Spanish	Boy Foreign	Total
Barcelona	2.4	10.2	4.5	14.8	4.7

Source: Author's elaboration from IIAB (2017); Based on data from the Departament d'Ensenyament de la Generalitat de Catalunya.

These poor results impact the possibility to continue after secondary compulsory school. Foreign 16-18-year-old pupils are over-represented among students choosing vocational professional paths and under-represented in the academic paths. There is a gender component as this is particularly true for foreign males and less marked for foreign females (IIAB, 2017) (See Table 2.7 and Table 2.8).

Table 2.7. Percentage of 16 to 18-year-old students registered in high- school (Bachillerato) by gender and nationality, 2015-2016, Barcelona

	Girl Spanish	Girl Foreign	Boy Spanish	Boy Foreign
Population 16-18	41.6	6.6	44	7.9
Bachillerato	48.3	4.8	43	3

Source: Reproduced from IIAB (2017); Based on data from Departament d'Estadistica de l'Ajuntament de Barcelona, Departament d'Ensenyament de la Generalitat de Catalunya.

Table 2.8. Students registered in vocational school, by nationality, 2015-2016, Barcelona

	Registered students 2015-2016	Foreign (%)
CFGM*	12 095	14.2
CFGS**	22 112	22.5

Note: CFGM= Formation Cycles of Medium Grade; **CFGM= Formation Cycles of Superior Grade
Source: Reproduced from IIAB (2017); Based on data from Departament d'Estadistica de l'Ajuntament de Barcelona, Departament d'Ensenyament de la Generalitat de Catalunya.

Local responses for migrant integration through education

Courses for adults

The municipality of Barcelona implements courses for migrants through two main channels. First, by directly co-implementing language courses with the Generalitat of Catalonia through the municipal Secretariat of Welcome Policies for Migrants. Second, the municipal Secretariat of Citizen's Rights and Diversity allocates subsidies to NGOs and migrant associations for the provision of complementary language courses and literacy classes for migrants.

Access to education for migrant children

In accordance with national prerogatives, access to public education is universal and compulsory for all children under 16 registered in the Padron, regardless of their legal status.

Education is regulated at the national level and provided at the regional level. In the case of Barcelona, the municipality is co-responsible (with the region) for providing education through the Consortium of Education, as they co-finance, co-design and co-implement primary and secondary education (See page 48). The municipality oversees kindergartens. Through the reception mechanisms (SAIER, SOAPI, New Families), the municipality provides information to newcomers about the educational system to ensure that migrant children have equal access to public education and that parents understand the system.

Responding to the increase in foreign pupils (from 3% in 2000 to around 12% in 2016 - reaching 22% in the public school system) and their specific needs, the Consortium has implemented since 2007 "Welcome classes" in public schools with high concentrations of foreign pupils. Recently-arrived pupils have tailor-made programmes for a few hours per day and the rest of the day they are integrated into regular classes. Welcome classes last two or three years depending on the difficulties of the pupils and contain, as well, psychological support and interaction with the families to help them understand the local school system. There are around 150 Welcome classes in the city (CEB, 2016; 2016b). The co- funding of Welcome Classes in the framework of the Education Consortium safeguarded them from budget cuts during the financial crisis. Parent associations (AMPA) in each school are responsible for schoolbooks when households cannot afford them. However, not all schools have active AMPAs and schools in disadvantaged neighbourhoods tend to have fewer AMPAs (e.g. Ciutat Vella, Nou Barris) (IIAB, 2017).

In addition, understanding integration as a two-way process, the Education Consortium has adapted school programmes for all children to diversity and geared toward young children. They encourage pupils to interact with each other in diverse settings.

Further, the municipality "Immigration department" organises, through the New Families programme, activities targeting school-age migrants to support their integration outside the classroom, including support for 12-18-year-old teenagers during the school year and an enrolment dropout prevention campaign. Through the programme "In summer, Barcelona Welcomes You", recently-arrived teenage migrants can participate in language, cultural and urban activities during the summer to build their confidence before the beginning of the academic year.

Notes

[1] http://ec.europa.eu/transparency/regdoc/rep/3/2015/EN/3-2015-5328-EN-F1-2-ANNEX-1.PDF

[2] http://ajuntament.barcelona.cat/estrategiaifinances/pressupostobert/ca/politicas#view=functional

[3] In 2015, 45% of the users were undocumented migrants (SAIER, 2016).

[4] https://bcnroc.ajuntament.barcelona.cat/jspui/bitstream/11703/102541/5/MGIrregularitat_3.pdf

[5] In 2013, 20% of Ciutat Meridiana apartments were involved in eviction proceedings (Darribau and Bhandar, 2016).

[6] The new municipal action plan can be found here:
http://habitatge.barcelona/sites/default/files/documents/pdhb_volum_ii_pla_pel_dret_a_lhabitatge_2016-2025.pdf

References

ACCEM-ECRE (2017), *AIDA: Asylum Information Database - Country report : Spain*, www.asylumineurope.org/sites/default/files/report-download/aida_es_2016update.pdf.

AB; Ajuntament de Barcelona. (AB) (2017a), *Barcelona Data Sheet 2017: Main economic indicators for the Barcelona Area*, Barcelona Activa, Barcelona, http://w42.bcn.cat/web/en/media-room/presentacions/index.jsp?componente=222-122538.

AB; Ajuntament de Barcelona (2017b), *L'economia de Barcelona 2016*, Gabinet Tècnic de Programació, Departament d'Estudis i Programació, Barcelona, http://ajuntament.barcelona.cat/barcelonaeconomia/sites/default/files/Informe%20anual%202016.pdf.

AB; Ajuntament de Barcelona (2017c), *El treball assalariat a Barcelona 2015: temporalitat, intensitat laboral i durada dels contractes, Departament d'estudis i Programacio*, Gabinet Tecnic de Programacio, Barcelona, https://bcnroc.ajuntament.barcelona.cat/jspui/bitstream/11703/101853/1/El%20treball%20assalariat%20a%20Barcelona%202015.pdf.

Ajuntament de Barcelona (AB) (2017d) Mesura de govern per garantir els drets de les persones en situación irregular, https://bcnroc.ajuntament.barcelona.cat/jspui/bitstream/11703/102541/5/MGIrregularitat_3.pdf

AB; Ajuntament de Barcelona (2016a), *Informes Estadistics: La poblacio estrangera a Barcelona: Gener 2016*, Departament d'Estadistica and Gabinet tecnic de Programacio, Barcelona, www.bcn.cat/estadistica/catala/dades/inf/pobest/pobest16/pobest16.pdf.

AB; Ajuntament de Barcelona (2016b), *Government measure: Municipal plan to combat Islamophobia*, Area of Rights, Participation and Transparency, Barcelona, www.uclg-cisdp.org/sites/default/files/Municipal%20Measure%20to%20combat%20Islamophobia.pdf.

AB; Ajuntament de Barcelona (2016c), *Distribución Territorial de la Renda per Càpita a Barcelona 2015*, Gabinet Tècnic de Programació, Departament d'Estudis i Programació, Barcelona, http://ajuntament.barcelona.cat/barcelonaeconomia/sites/default/files/RFD_2015_BCN.pdf.

AB; Ajuntament de Barcelona (2015), *Pla per el Dret a l'Habitatge 2016-2025*, Regidoría d'Habitatge, Barcelona, http://habitatge.barcelona/sites/default/files/documents/1_analisi_i_diagnosi_fi.pdf.

AB; Ajuntament de Barcelona (2014), *Enquesta de valors socials 2014*, Departament d'Estudis d'Opinio and Gabinet Tecnic de Porgramacio, Barcelona, https://bcnroc.ajuntament.barcelona.cat/jspui/bitstream/11703/99225/4/r14033_Valors%20Socials_En creuaments.pdf.

AB; Ajuntament de Barcelona (2012), *Plan de Trabajo de Inmigracion 2012-2015*, AB, Barcelona, www.bcn.cat/novaciutadania/pdf/pla_immigracio/pla_immigracio_es.pdf.

Ajuntament de Barcelona (AB). (2010). Pla Barcelona Interculturalitat, Barcelona

AB; Ajuntament de Barcelona (2008), *Pla de Treball d'Immigracio 2008-2011*, Consell Municipal d'Immigració de Barcelona, Barcelona, www.bcn.cat/novaciutadania/pdf/ca/participacio/programes/valoraciopladetreball08-11.pdf.

Ajuntament de Barcelona (AB) (2008b). Informes Estadistics: La poblacio estrangera a Barcelona: Gener 2008, Departament d'Estadistica, Gabinet tecnic de Programacio, Barcelona

Ajuntament de Barcelona (AB). (2004). La poblacio esrtangera a Barcelona, Gener 2004, Departament d'Estadistica, Barcelona

Alvarez Enriquez, L. (2013), "Interculturalidad: Inclusion y exclusion en la politica de gestion de la diversidad en Barcelona", *La Revista del CLAD Reforma y Democracia*, 57, Caracas, http://siare.clad.org/fulltext/0074000.pdf.

AMB; Area Metropolitana de Barcelona (2015), *Anuari Metropolità de Barcelona 2015,* Institut d' Estudis Regionals i Metropolitans, Barcelona, https://iermb.uab.cat/ca/iermb/anuari/anuari-metropolita-de-barcelona-2015/.

AMB; Area Metropolitana de Barcelona (2014), *Anuari Metropolità de Barcelona 2014: Creixement inclusiu: el gran repte estratègic metropolità,* Institut d'Estudis Regionals i Metropolitans, Barcelona, www.amazon.com.br/ANUARI-METROPOLIT%C3%80-BARCELONA-2014-CREIXEMENT/dp/8492940190.

AMB; Area Metropolitana de Barcelona (2012), *Anuari Metropolità de Barcelona 2012: Bases per a una nova estrategia Metropolitana Económica i Social,* Institut d' Estudis Regionals i Metropolitans, Barcelona, https://issuu.com/ambcomunicacio/docs/bases_per_a_una_nova_estrat_gia_me.

Bayona y Carrasco, J. and A. Lopez Gay (2011), "Concentración, segregación y movilidad residencial de los extranjeros en Barcelona", *Documentos d'Anàlisis Geogràfica*, 57/3, pp. 381-412.

Bayona y Carrasco, J. and M. Rubiales Perez (2015), "La inmigración internacional en Barcelona, Madrid y sus respectivas metrópolis", in *Barcelona y Madrid : Procesos urbanos y dinámicas sociale,* Geografía y Urbanismo , Madrid.

Boulant, J., M. Brezzi and P. Veneri (2016), "Income levels and inequality in metropolitan areas: A comparative approach in OECD countries"

Cano Fuentes G., A. Etxezarreta Etxarri, D. Kees, and J. Hoekstra (2013), "From housing bubble to repossessions: Spain compared to other South-European countries", *Housing Studies*, 28/8, pp.1197-1217, https://doi.org/10.1080/02673037.2013.818622.

Castles, S. (2004), "Globalización e Inmigración", in *Inmigración y procesos de cambio*, Icaria, Barcelona.

CEAR (2017), "Mas que cifras - Dados y Estdísticas de asilo de 2017", www.masquecifras.org/, (accessed September 2017).

CIIMU-Institut Infancia I Món Urbà (2013), Avaluació del programa d'acompanyament al reagrupament familiar a Barcelona – Informe Final

Charbit, C. (2011), "Governance of Public Policies in Decentralised Contexts: The Multi-level approach", *OECD Regional Development Working Papers*, 2011/04, OECD Publishing, Paris.

Charbit, C. and M. Michalun (2009), "Mind the gaps: Managing Mutual Dependence in Relations among Levels of Government", *OECD Working Papers on Public Governance*, No. 14, OECD Publishing, Paris. doi:10.1787/221253707200

Consorci d'Educacio de Barcelona (CEB). (2016). L'escolaritzacio a la ciutat de Barcelona – Curs 2014-2015, Recull estadistic, Generalitat de Catalunya, Ajuntament de Barcelona

Consorci d'Educacio de Barcelona (CEB). (2016b). Memoria d'activitats 2014-2015, Generalitat de Catalunya, Ajutnament de Barcelona

Darribau, D. and B. Bhandar (2016), "Foreclosed city: A Barcelona neighbourhood Unites to fight evictions", *World Policy Journal*, 33/1, pp.58-69, https://muse.jhu.edu/article/613177/pdf.

Diaz Ramirez, Marcos, Liebig Thomas, Cécile Thoreau and Paolo Veneri, (2018). "The integration of migrants in OECD regions: A first assessment," OECD Regional Development Working Papers 2018/01, OECD Publishing.

European Commission (2016), *Quality of life in European cities 2015*, Regional and Urban Policy, Bruxelles, http://ec.europa.eu/regional_policy/sources/docgener/studies/pdf/urban/survey2015_en.pdf.

Generalitat de Catalunya. (2014). Equitat I resultat de l'alumnat estranger a PISA 2012, Consell Superior d'Avaluacio Del Sistema Educatiu, Departament d'Ensenyament

Gimenez, C. (2003), "Pluralismo, multiculturalismo e interculturalidad: propuesta de clarificacion y apuntes educativos", in *Educacion y Futuro: Revista de Investigacion Aplicada y Experiencias Educativas*, 8, pp. 9-26, http://red.pucp.edu.pe/ridei/wp-content/uploads/biblioteca/100416.pdf.

Gonzalez-Enriquez, C. (2009), *Undocumented migration: counting the uncountable - Data and trends across Europe: Country report Spain*, European Comission, www.eliamep.gr/en/category/migration/.

Guell, B. et al. (2017), *Resum de la diagnosi del comerç pakistanès al barri del Raval*, Barcelona Activa, Barcelona, https://media-edg.barcelona.cat/wp-content/uploads/2017/07/27151852/Resum-comerc%CC%A7-pakistane%CC%80s_FINAL.pdf.

Guiraudon, V. (2009), *The multi-level governance of international migration : an unbalanced act?*, http://cor.europa.eu/en/activities/governance/documents/ed907180-8673-4101-90e3-16b9927eceb0.pdf.

Idescat; Institut d'Estadística de Catalunya (2016), *Municipal Padron* (database).

IERMB (2017) Creixament inclusiu urbà : EL creixement inclusiu des d'una perspectiva urbana : un repte per a la metrópoli de Barcelona

IERMB (2018), *Anuari Metropolità de Barcelona 2017*, https://iermb.uab.cat/ca/publicacions/anuari-metropolita-de-barcelona/.

IERMB (2017), *Creixament inclusiu urbà : EL creixement inclusiu des d'una perspectiva urbana : un repte per a la metrópoli de Barcelona*, https://iermb.uab.cat/wp-content/uploads/2018/02/17032.pdf.

IERMB-AMB-DIBA-IDESCAT (2014), *Crisi econòmica, creixement de les desigualtats i transformacions socials : Informe general Enquesta de Condicions de Vida i Hàbits de la població de Catalunya 2011*, www.researchgate.net/profile/Sergio_Porcel2/publication/282777558_Transformacions_familiars_me tropolitanitzacio_i_cohesio_social_els_efectes_de_la_suburbanitzacio_barcelonina_en_la_diferenciac io_de_les_dinamiques_familiars_i_la_cura_d%27infants/links/561bfb0a08ae044edbb38c5b/Transfor macions-familiars-metropolitanitzacio-i-cohesio-social-els-efectes-de-la-suburbanitzacio-barcelonina-en-la-diferenciacio-de-les-dinamiques-familiars-i-la-cura-dinfants.pdf.

IIAB; Institut Infancia I Adolescencia de Barcelona (2017), *Oportunitats educatives a Barcelona 2016 : l'educacio de la infancia I l'adolescencia a la ciutat*, http://institutinfancia.cat/wp-content/uploads/2017/04/20170407_oportunitatseducativesbcn2016-1.pdf.

INE; Instituto Nacional de Estadística (2017), *Municipal Padron* (database).

INE (n.d.), *Survey of Active Population* (database).

Martinez, U. (1999), *Pobreza, segregación y exclusión espacial,* Icaria, Barcelona.

Massey, D. S. (1985), "Ethnic residential segregation: a theoretical synthesis and empirical review", *Sociology and social research*, 69, pp. 315-350, www.popline.org/node/412371.

OECD (2018a), *Working together for local migrant and refugee integration,* OECD publications, Paris, http://dx.doi.org/10.1787/9789264085350-en.

OECD (2018b) Subnational governmnets in OECD countries, Key data http://www.oecd.org/regional/regional-policy/Subnational-governments-in-OECD-Countries-Key-Data-2018.pdf

OECD (2016), *International Migration Outlook 2016*, OECD Publishing, Paris, http://dx.doi.org/10.1787/migr_outlook-2016-en.

OECD (2010a), *Higher Education in Regional and City Development: The Autonomous Region of Catalonia, Spain*, OECD Publishing, Paris, www.oecd.org/education/imhe/46826969.pdf.

OECD (2010b), *Organising Local Economic Development: The Role of Development Agencies and Companies*, OECD Publishing, Paris, http://dx.doi.org/10.1787/9789264083530-en.

OECD (2009), *Promoting Entrepreneurship, Employment and Business Competitiveness: the Experience of Barcelona*, OECD Publishing, Paris, www.oecd.org/cfe/leed/43505170.pdf.

OECD-European Union (2015), *Indicators of Immigrant Integration 2015: Settling In*, OECD Publishing, Paris, www.oecd.org/els/mig/Indicators-of-Immigrant-Integration-2015.pdf.

Pareja-Eastaway, M. (2009), "The effects of the Spanish housing system on the settlement patterns of immigrants", *Tijdschrift voor Economische on Sociale Geogroafie*, 100/4, pp. 519 – 534, https://onlinelibrary.wiley.com/doi/pdf/10.1111/j.1467-9663.2009.00556.x.

SAIER (2016), *Memoria del Servei d'Atencio a Immigrants, Emigrants I Refugiats*, www.bcn.cat/novaciutadania/pdf/saier/SAIER.memoria.2016_ca.pdf.

Salvi del Pero, A. et al (2016), "Policies to promote access to good-quality affordable housing in OECD countries", *OECD Social, Employment and Migration Working Papers*, 176, OECD Publishing, Paris, http://dx.doi.org/10.1787/1815199X.

Schnapper, D. (2007), *Qu'est-ce que l'intégration?* Folio Actuel – Gallimard, Paris.

Schneider,F. (2010), *The influence of the Economic crisis on the underground economy in Germany and the other OECD countries in 2010: a (further) increase*, www.econ.jku.at/members/Schneider/files/publications/LatestResearch2010/ShadEcOECD2010.pdf.

Scholten. P. (2014), "The multilevel Governance of migrant integration, Migration: A COMPAS Anthology", in *Migration: A COMPAS Anthology*, COMPAS, Oxford.

Scholten, P. and R. Penninx (2016), "The multi-level governance of Migration and Integration", in *Integration processes and policies in Europe*, IMISCOE, Rotterdam.

Serra del Pozo, P. (2006), *El comercio etnico en el districto de Ciutat Vella*, Fundacio La Caixa, Barcelona, https://pauserra.files.wordpress.com/2008/08/pau-serra-el-comercio-etnico-en-el-distrito-de-ciutat-vella.pdf.

Spencer, S. (2017). 'Multi-level governance of an intractable policy problem: migrants with irregular status in Europe'. *Journal of Ethnic and Migration Studies.*

Statistics of Barcelona (2016), *Municipal Padron* (database).

Subdelegacio del Govern a Barcelona. (2017). Memoria 2016: Oficina d'Estrangeria Barcelona, Solicitudes Presentadas. Proteccion internacional

UNSD (2017), "International migration statistics", United Nations Statistics Division, https://unstats.un.org/unsd/demographic/sconcerns/migration/migrmethods.htm#B.

Zapata, R. (2015). "Intercultural policy and multi-level governance in Barcelona: mainstreaming comprehensive approach", *International Review of Administrative Sciences*, pp. 1-20, http://journals.sagepub.com/doi/abs/10.1177/0020852315592962.

Further Reading

Area Metropolitana de Barcelona. (AMB) (2011). Anuari Metropolità de Barcelona 2011: Per afrontar la crisi: la Metropoli de Barcelona, Institut d' Estudis Regionals i Metropolitans, Barcelona

Gebhardt, D. (2014). Building Inclusive Cities: Challenges in the Multilevel Governance of Immigrant Integration in Europe, A report for Migration Policy Institute

Observatorio Espanol del Racismo y la Xenofobia (OERX). (2012). Evolucion del racismo y la xenofobia en Espana, Informe 2012

OECD (2016), Making cities work for all: data and actions for inclusive growth, OECD Publishing, Paris, https://doi.org/10.1787/9789264263260-en.

OECD (2018) Divided cities: Understanding Inter-urban Inequalities, OECD Publishing, Paris, https://doi.org/10.1787/9789264300385-en.

Zapata, R. (2005). Inmigracion, un desafio para Espana, Madrid Editorial Pablo Iglesisas

Annex A. List of participants in the meetings held in Barcelona with the OECD team – 3rd- 4th - 5th April 2017

Central Government and Spanish Sub-delegation in Barcelona

- Ablanedo, E. Deputy Delegate of the National Government Sub-Delegation in Barcelona. Interviewed by: OECD delegation. (Tuesday 4th April 2017).

- Diego, E. Director of the Foreign Office of Barcelona. Interviewed by: OECD delegation. (Tuesday 4th April 2017).

- Garcia- Villar, F. Sub-director general of Migrant Integration at the Spanish Ministry of Employment and Social Security. Interviewed by: OECD delegation. (Tuesday 4th April 2017)

Autonomous Community: Generalitat of Catalonia

- Amorós, O. Secretary of Equality, Migration and Citizenship at the Department of Employment and Social Affairs of the Generalitat of Catalonia. Interviewed by: OECD delegation. (Tuesday 4th April 2017).

- Domingo, M. at the Consortium of Education of Barcelona. Interviewed by: OECD delegation. (Wednesday 5th April 2017).

Municipality: Barcelona city council

- Asens, J. Deputy Mayor in charge of Citizenship Rights, Participation and Transparency at the Barcelona City Hall. Interviewed by: OECD delegation. (Monday 3rd April 2017)

- Calbó, I. Director of the programme Barcelona Refugee City at the Barcelona City Hall. Interviewed by: OECD delegation. (Monday 3rd April 2017)

- Guillen, A. Director of Servicez for Citizenship and Immigration Rights at the Barcelona City Hall. Interviewed by: OECD delegation. (Tuesday 4th April 2017).

- Jou, E. Housing Deputy Director at the Barcelona City Council. Interviewed by: OECD delegation. (Wednesday 5th April 2017).

- Rendón, G. Coordinator of *SAIER*-Attention Services for Migrants and Refugees at the Barcelona City Hall. Interviewed by: OECD delegation. (Monday 3rd April 2017)

- Sanahuja, R. Director of *SAIER*-Attention Services for Migrants and Refugees at the Barcelona City Hall. Interviewed by: OECD delegation. (Monday 3rd April 2017)

- Ventura, L. Director of the Transversal Programme of Barcelona Activa at the Barcelona City Hall. Interviewed by: OECD delegation. (Wednesday 5th April 2017).

NGOs and Civil Society organisations

- Ahmed, F. Dialegs de la dona. Interviewed by: OECD delegation. (Tuesday 4th April 2017).

- Alaiz, E. Fundación Migra studium, Coordinadora de la Llengüa. Interviewed by: OECD delegation. (Tuesday 4th April 2017).

- Avinyoa, B. Centre Exil. Interviewed by: OECD delegation. (Tuesday 4th April 2017).

- Bitani, M. Political refugee and journalist from Siria. Interviewed by: OECD delegation. (Tuesday 4th April 2017).

- Coissard, P. Catalan Commission for Refugees. Interviewed by: OECD delegation. (Tuesday 4th April 2017).

- Fatou, N. Cooperative Jamcop. Interviewed by: OECD delegation. (Tuesday 4th April 2017).

- Garcia Bonomi, J. Fedelatina. Interviewed by: OECD delegation. (Tuesday 4th April 2017).

- Losa, B. Associació Catalana per a la Integració d'Homosexuals, Bisexuals i Transsexuals Immigrants (ACATHI). Interviewed by: OECD delegation. (Tuesday 4th April 2017).

- Mataix, T. Consortium of Linguistic Normalisation. Interviewed by: OECD delegation. (Monday 3rd April 2017)

Were also interviewed: Members of the partner NGO´s working in the SAIER: AMIC and Col.legi d'Advocats de Barcelona. Interviewed by: OECD delegation. (Monday 3rd April 2017). Also, members of other non-governmental organisations: Plataforma per la LLengua, Red Solidaria and the International Criminal Bar. Interviewed by: OECD delegation. (Tuesday 4th April 2017).

Annex B. Division of competences for integration relevant matters across levels of government

Spain is a decentralised country with three tiers of sub-national governments each of them with specific competences. Along with the national government (1) Autonomous Communities (CA), (2) Provinces and (3) Municipalities hold specific administrative competences as well as decision and management autonomy. The *Government delegations* are territorialised representations of the central government in autonomous regions and within them, the Government Sub-delegations are territorialised representations of the central government in provinces.

Along with the national government, there are 17 Autonomous Communities with executive and legislative powers. The Autonomous Community of Catalonia is governed by the Generalitat of Catalonia. The democratic transition lead to an open-ended model of territorial organisation and the seventeen Autonomous Communities (CA) have asymmetric powers. The Generalitat of Catalonia has a Parliament which can legislate within the framework of the Generalitat competences, and an elected government composed by autonomous "departments" directed by councillors. The competencies and financing system of Catalonia and its relationship with Spain are defined in the Autonomy Statute (2006) in the framework of the Spanish Constitution. Matters not expressly assigned to the central government by the Constitution may fall under the jurisdiction of Autonomous Communities by virtue of the Statutes of Autonomy. Competences not claimed by Statutes of Autonomy fall with the State, whose laws shall prevail, in case of conflict, over those of the Autonomous Communities regarding all matters in which exclusive jurisdiction has not been conferred upon the latter.

Within each Autonomous Community there are provinces. In Catalonia, there are four provinces, one of them is Barcelona which is almost equivalent to the metropolitan region around the city of Barcelona. Neither the provincial (Diputación) and metropolitan bodies (Area Metropolitana de Barcelona) have competences in terms of migration nor implement policies about it.

The cities of Barcelona and Madrid have a special regime compared to the other municipalities: since the establishment of the Chart of Barcelona (1998), several competences are assigned to the local authority or under shared jurisdiction between the municipality and the Generalitat.

National level – The Central Government

Ministry of Employment and Social Security

Defines national policy for migration and migrant integration

Regulation of migration flows and administers migration permits

Implements asylum seekers social protection programme and accommodation facilities in collaboration with partner NGOs

Employment policy and unemployment allowances

Ministry of Interior

Administers right to asylum

Sub-delegation of the national government in Catalonia- Foreigns Office

Migrant admissions

Ministry of Health

National guide lines for health policy

Ministry of Justice

Nationality procedures

Autonomous Community – The Generalitat of Catalonia

Competences over health, education, social services, transport and communication, culture, local economic development, agriculture and energy, urban planning and civil protection, employment, Language Learning and Unaccompanied Minors

Metropolitan Area of Barcelona – AMB

Competences over mobility and transport, urban planning and environment

Municipality of Barcelona

Competences over urban planning, public transport, social services (including shelter for homeless and social issues in the public space), education, health, social housing and culture, Local register (*Padrón*), language learning, Welcoming policies for migrants

Associations

Accommodation facilities for asylum seeker; Language courses; reception support; Social Action; Intercultural programs, civic engagement .

ORGANISATION FOR ECONOMIC CO-OPERATION AND DEVELOPMENT

The OECD is a unique forum where governments work together to address the economic, social and environmental challenges of globalisation. The OECD is also at the forefront of efforts to understand and to help governments respond to new developments and concerns, such as corporate governance, the information economy and the challenges of an ageing population. The Organisation provides a setting where governments can compare policy experiences, seek answers to common problems, identify good practice and work to co-ordinate domestic and international policies.

The OECD member countries are: Australia, Austria, Belgium, Canada, Chile, the Czech Republic, Denmark, Estonia, Finland, France, Germany, Greece, Hungary, Iceland, Ireland, Israel, Italy, Japan, Korea, Latvia, Lithuania, Luxembourg, Mexico, the Netherlands, New Zealand, Norway, Poland, Portugal, the Slovak Republic, Slovenia, Spain, Sweden, Switzerland, Turkey, the United Kingdom and the United States. The European Union takes part in the work of the OECD.

OECD Publishing disseminates widely the results of the Organisation's statistics gathering and research on economic, social and environmental issues, as well as the conventions, guidelines and standards agreed by its members.

OECD PUBLISHING, 2, rue André-Pascal, 75775 PARIS CEDEX 16

(85 2018 14 1 P) ISBN 978-92-64-30405-5 – 2018